These are perilous times for the Church. For years, we have been struggling under the weight of bold lies that are tearing at the fabric of our families, our churches, and our nation. Ken Ham understands this and knows that the only antidote to a bold lie is bold truth. In *Divided Nation,* Mr. Ham outlines the issues with biblical clarity and calls Christians back to a place of biblical authority. Every committed Christian needs a copy of this timely book!

Heidi St. John

Author, Speaker, Host of "Off the Bench" with Heidi St. John and Founder of MomStrongInternational.com

Every day it seems our American culture descends further away from the blessing and protection we once enjoyed. Many in the Church, pastors and congregants alike, are unsure how to address the anti-God ideas sweeping politics, education, family, entertainment, social media, and every other sphere of society. This book exposes a root of the problem and offers a strong, biblical solution.

Kirk Cameron

Actor & producer

Unless America changes course she is heading toward catastrophe. Ken Ham's book *Divided Nation* takes a close look at what is ailing our culture today and what to do about it. Thankfully, this powerful, insightful, and practical book tells how we can get back to the authority of God's Word, which answers every dilemma of life.

Jack Hibbs

Chino Hills, California

I cannot think of a more timely book for the current predicament that we find ourselves in — both as a nation, and as the Church. From the first chapter to the last, Ken Ham masterfully diagnosis the crippling problems that are plaguing both America and the Body of Christ. And more importantly, he gives clear, biblical marching orders for those who are called to be "the light of the world" and "the salt of the earth." But what makes this book extraordinarily powerful is that the author does more than preach the riveting message found in its pages, he lives it — loud and clear. Prepare to be shaken, awakened, and inspired to do the same.

Emeal ("E.Z.") Zwayne

President, Living Waters

DIVIDED✝NATION

CULTURES IN CHAOS & A CONFLICTED CHURCH

KEN HAM

First printing: June 2021
Sixth printing: January 2024

ISBN: 978-1-68344-283-7
ISBN: 978-1-61458-778-1
Library of Congress Number: 2021937297

Cover by Diana Bogardus

Unless otherwise noted, Scripture quotations are from the English Standard Version (ESV) of the Bible.

Please consider requesting that a copy of this volume be purchased by your local library system.

Printed in the United States of America

Please visit our website for other great titles:
www.masterbooks.com

For information regarding promotional opportunities, please contact the publicity department at pr@nlpg.com.

Master
Books®
A Division of New Leaf Publishing Group
www.masterbooks.com

Contents

■ INTRODUCTION

I have a burden to help the church equip God's people to defend the Christian faith, proclaim the gospel with boldness in a way people will listen to and understand, and raise up godly generations who will continue a godly legacy generation after generation.

Many people in the church today are perplexed at what is happening to the culture and in the church with the exodus of the younger generations. Christians in the West are increasingly looked on as the enemy, and persecution is increasing.

In this book I attempt to explain what has happened to the church and culture and examine what we as God's people can do about the situation.

This book really represents what we call the "relevance talk" that I give to God's people. Throughout the book are illustrations I use in such a talk. I am making all these illustrations and more available as PDFs, Keynote, or PowerPoint slides for people to use them. I encourage pastors, other Christian leaders, or anyone with a heart for reaching people with the truth of God's Word and the gospel to use these slides and teach the content of this book to as many as possible.

The illustrations are available for free at this link: answersingenesis.org/go/nation.

I pray the message of this book will be spread far and wide and will help bring a needed new reformation and revival in our nation.

Also, I want to thank Answers in Genesis staff members:

Avery Foley for her editing skills.

Maria Suter and Cameron Suter for using their artistic talents in producing the illustrations.

— Ken Ham

Chapter One

A DIVIDED NATION

America is a divided nation. Then again, what's happening in America is also happening throughout the Western world. The culture is becoming more secularized and anti-Christian. Church attendance has already dropped significantly. But what has happened to the church? Why have the younger generations been leaving? Why is the Christian message not impacting the culture like it used to?

An Exodus from the Church

Now, don't misunderstand me. God's Word states, *I will build my church, and the gates of hell shall not prevail against it* (Matthew 16:18). There are some great Christian leaders, pastors, and others who stand boldly and courageously for the authority of the Word of God. But, sadly, they are a minority. One of

7

the most-asked questions I receive through email and letters and from visitors to the Ark Encounter and Creation Museum attractions is something like this: "Do you know a church in our area that takes the same stand on biblical authority as you do at Answers in Genesis?"

From an institutional (local) church perspective, there has been a problem in much of the church in America and the rest of the Western world. For many, many years now, we've seen an exodus of young people from the church. I've been talking on this ever since the '70s. In fact, I gave my first talk on creation apologetics in 1975 in Australia. During the early '80s I visited America, giving talks across the nation in churches and Christian institutions. One of the things I was saying back then went something like this:

> *If the church doesn't raise up generations to believe God's Word starting in Genesis and understand Genesis 1 to 11 as literal history and the foundation for all of our doctrine, for our whole worldview, for the rest of the Bible, for the gospel, and for everything. . . .*
>
> *And if the church doesn't equip generations with answers to the secular attacks on God's Word, and specifically Genesis, that they are*

getting through the education system and the media. . . .

And if the church doesn't stop compromising God's Word in Genesis, with evolution and/or millions of years as so many (including many church leaders and academics) in our churches sadly do. . . .

Then we will lose the coming generations, and we'll lose the culture.

And that's exactly what's happening right before our very eyes.

It Only Takes One Generation

It only takes one generation to lose a culture. We're seeing a once very "Christianized" America on the brink of catastrophic change from a Christian worldview perspective. The younger generations (particularly Generation Y [millennials] and Generation Z) are growing up in a very different culture than the culture my generation (baby boomers) and older generations grew up in. The change in the culture is devastating and catastrophic from a Christian perspective.

Christians need to be aware of what's happening and how to deal with this. But much of the church is not giving the teaching to understand why the culture is at the place it is and how to deal with it.

In this book I am going to detail five areas where I believe many parents and church leaders have failed to teach people to equip them for the fallen world in which we live.

I believe there has been an overall neglect of and failure to teach:

1. There is no neutral position.
2. There is no non-religious position.
3. There are ultimately only two religions — two foundations for our worldview.
4. General Bible and creation apologetics.
5. How to think foundationally to develop a truly Christian worldview.

Further on, I will explain each of these in detail to help us understand what sort of teaching needs to be included in the church and in parenting in order to raise up godly generations.

In 2009 I co-authored the book *Already Gone*. It's still as relevant today as it was then. We contracted with America's Research Group, and they surveyed young people, particularly millennials, who used to go to church but no longer go to church. Research had shown that two-thirds of young people were leaving the church by college age, with very few returning, and we wanted to find out why they left the church.

When these young people were asked, "Why did you leave church?" the answers really came down to issues like this:

How can you believe in a loving God with all the death and suffering in the world?
What about science and the Bible?
Can you really trust the Bible in a scientific age?
What about evolution and millions of years?

Now over 90% of kids from church homes in the USA have been sent to the public education system, and we have to be honest about it. What's happened is that system has progressively changed to become more and more atheistic. By and large, public school educators have thrown out God, the Bible, Christian prayer, and Genesis and creation. As a result, many now claim they threw religion out. But that's not true. They threw Christianity out and replaced it with a different religion.

Chapter Two

THERE IS NO NEUTRALITY

My first point is:

1. There is no neutral position.

This is a problem in the church today. There's been a failure within much of the church to teach generations to understand that there is no neutrality — no neutral position.

Let's look at what God's Word clearly teaches us.

- One is either for Christ or against Him. One either gathers or scatters: *Whoever is not with me is against me, and whoever does not gather with me scatters* (Matthew 12:30).
- One either walks in light or darkness: ...*For at one time you were darkness, but now you are light in the Lord. Walk as children of light* (Ephesians 5:8).

13

- One is either on the broad way or narrow way: *Enter by the narrow gate. For the gate is wide and the way is easy that leads to destruction, and those who enter by it are many. For the gate is narrow and the way is hard that leads to life, and those who find it are few* (Matthew 7:13–14).

- One either builds their house on the rock or the sand: *Everyone then who hears these words of mine and does them will be like a wise man who built his house on the rock. . . . And everyone who hears these words of mine and does not do them will be like a foolish man who built his house on the sand* (Matthew 7:24–26).

- One not for God is hostile to God: *For the mind that is set on the flesh is hostile to God, for it does not submit to God's law; indeed, it cannot* (Romans 8:7).

- One who is not righteous is unrighteous and suppresses truth: *For in it the righteousness of God is revealed from faith to faith, as it is written, "The righteous shall live by faith." For the wrath of God is revealed from heaven against all ungodliness and unrighteousness of men, who by their unrighteousness suppress the truth. For what can be known about God is plain to them, because God has shown it to them* (Romans 1:17–19).

There are many more passages that deal with this topic, but Scripture makes it clear there is no neutral position. Man is not neutral because the Bible says *for all have sinned*

(Romans 3:23) and that *The heart is deceitful above all things, and desperately sick; who can understand it?* (Jeremiah 17:9).

Public Education Is Not Neutral

So educators and legislators who removed any Christian teaching, the Bible, or prayer from public schools did not make a neutral decision. And if the education system is not for Christ, it is against Him. As we will better understand later, the public education system, by and large, is now an atheistic system, as everything is explained in terms of natural processes (naturalism). Naturalism (no supernatural is involved) is atheism. This is a system of belief based on the idea that man by himself can determine truth. And because the system is not for Christ, it is against Him.

Generations of kids (over 90% of those from church homes) have attended the secular education system. Many Christian leaders, even in conservative churches, have encouraged the kids to go to that system where now they're being trained in an atheistic worldview with the foundation that man determines truth. The justification is often given that children are to be salt and witness in that system. But as I state in my book *Will They Stand*, they can't be salt until they have salt in themselves (Mark 9:50), and if the salt is contaminated, it is good for nothing (Matthew 5:13). Most children and young people have not been equipped in their homes and church to have the right foundation for a truly Christian worldview, to know what they believe and why, and taught apologetics to be able to defend the Christian faith against secular attacks. Most succumb to the increasing atheistic indoctrination (e.g., in naturalistic evolution/millions of years) and begin to doubt the Bible, particularly when it comes to Genesis. This opens the door for them to be brainwashed into accepting moral relativism as they're indoctrinated to conform to the world's acceptance of LGBTQ+, abortion, critical race theory, and so on.

Then they're coming back to their homes, churches, Sunday schools, and youth groups with many questions about the Bible that have resulted in doubt and disbelief in regard to what the Bible teaches. You will recognize the questions because they are the same basic questions we hear from people all around the world today. Questions such as:

Don't we live in a scientific age?
Hasn't science disproved the Bible?
How do you know the Bible is true?
What evidence is there for God?
If there is a God, who made God?
You believe in Adam and Eve? Well, where did Cain get his wife?
How did the races come about if there were only two people to start with?
Where's the evidence of Noah's Flood?
Don't fossil layers prove millions of years in evolution?

*We know man evolved from apelike creatures, so how
	could the story of Adam and Eve be true?*

*How can you believe in a loving God with all the death
	and suffering we see in the world?*

*Didn't dinosaurs live millions of years ago and evolve
	into birds?*

How could Noah fit all the animals on the Ark?

Hasn't science proved evolution is true?

Isn't the Bible an outdated book of mythology?

Don't Muslims and Christians believe in the same God?

*What's wrong with gay "marriage" if two people love
	each other?*

And there are many more questions just like these.

Now what happens in a majority of instances — in homes, churches, Christian and Bible colleges, seminaries, etc. — is students are given an answer like this: "Don't worry about Genesis or many of those other questions. You can believe in evolution and millions of years. You can believe what you've been taught in school. Just trust in Jesus, Johnny."

Many atheists (and others) who grew up in church homes have testified that they asked their pastors or Sunday school teachers questions because of what they learned at school, but they didn't get answers and so they rejected the Christian faith. They start to realize that if the first part of the Bible is not true, how can the rest be true? Doubt leads to unbelief, and they leave the church.

What our research published in 2009 (in *Already Gone*) showed us can be summarized like this: Generations weren't taught apologetics; they weren't taught how to defend their faith; and they weren't taught a truly Christian worldview to know what they believe and why. Many were told they could add evolution and millions of years to the Bible and reinterpret Genesis. To them, this meant the Bible really can't be trusted.

What Does the Data Say?

Let's look at research data published in regard to church attendance for the past few generations. Researchers divide people into generations according to when they were born. Consider the research from the Pew Research Center (a secular research organization) in 2010:

Attendance at Religious Services by Generation; Percent saying they attend several times a week, every week, or nearly every week.[1]

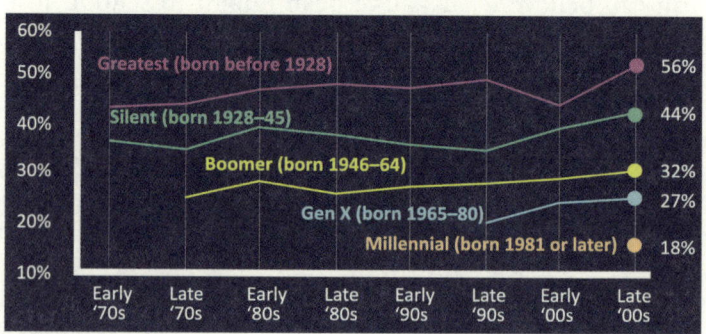

We observe that church attendance in America has dropped from 56% with the Greatest Generation to 18% for millennials. Now look at more recent research from the GSS Data Explorer website concerning USA church attendance. Although the groups don't mesh exactly with the Pew Research Center, this research shows what the more recent trends are as we begin to include some of Generation Z in the image below.

Generation Z is the name given to the generation after the millennials (or Gen Y). They are those born (different groups have slightly different ranges) between 1996 and 2015. The youngest generation (born after 2015) is called Generation Alpha.

Attendance at Religious Services by Generation; Percent saying they attend every week.[2]

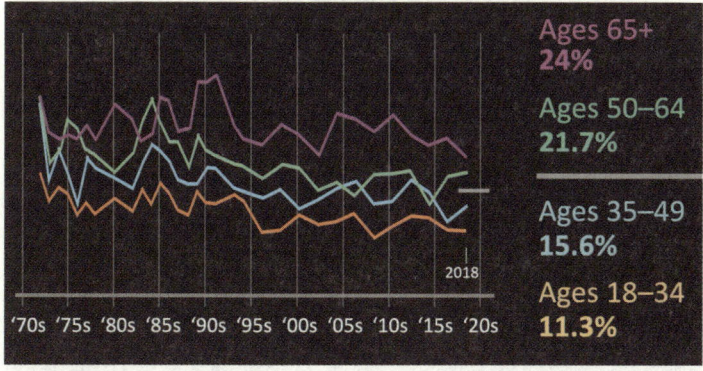

Enter Generation Z: Born between 1999 and 2015, they are the first truly "post-Christian" generation.[3]

In 2018, George Barna said his research on Gen Z shows that they are the first truly post-Christian generation. He found they were twice as likely to be atheist as any previous generation.

Those who are atheists think they are being neutral, having no religion. But as discussed, this is simply not true. They've been brainwashed into believing that the position they hold is supposedly proven by science. We have to do a lot of work with this group in teaching them how to think logically and to understand the true nature of science and its limitations when it comes to the origins issue.

U.S. Religious Identity 2018[4]
Which of the following best describes your religious faith?

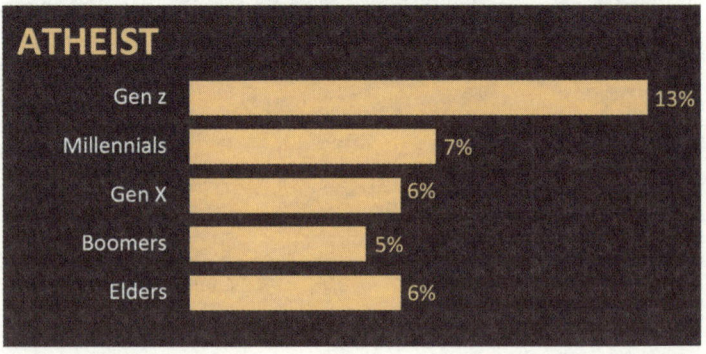

ATHEIST

Gen z	13%
Millennials	7%
Gen X	6%
Boomers	5%
Elders	6%

U.S. Religious Identity 2018[5]

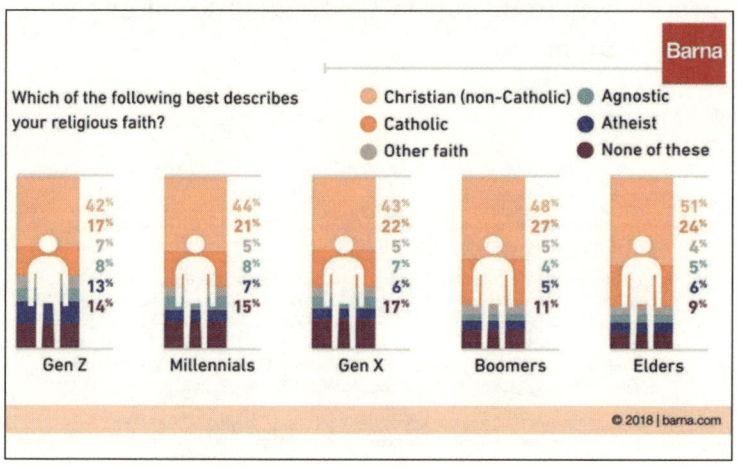

What Should We Do?

Parents: Carefully and prayerfully consider who is influencing your children. Public education is not neutral. Even Christian education can do more harm than good if those teaching, and the curricula used, aren't rooted in the truth of God's Word. For additional information on education and how to choose which education option is best for your family, read my book *Will They Stand*.

Pastors and parents: Fill your church or home library with solid apologetics resources for all ages and levels. Beware of Christian resources that do not uphold the authority of God's Word but teach compromise positions like theistic evolution. These resources are dangerous, leading people away from trust in God's Word to starting with man's word instead.

ENDNOTES

1 Pew Research Center, "Religion Among the Millennials," A Pew Forum on Religion & Public Life Report, February 2010, 7.

2 Smith, Tom W., Davern, Michael, Freese, Jeremy, and Morgan, Stephen, General Social Surveys, 1972–2018 [machine-readable data file] /Principal Investigator, Smith, Tom W.; Co-Principal Investigators, Michael Davern, Jeremy Freese, and Stephen Morgan Sponsored by National Science Foundation. — NORC ed. — Chicago: NORC, 2018: NORC at the University of Chicago [producer and distributor]. Data accessed from the GSS Data Explorer website at gssdataexplorer.norc.org. Accessed January 7, 2021.

3 "Atheism Doubles Among Generation Z," Barna, January 24, 2018, https://www.barna.com/research/atheism-doubles-among-generation-z/.

4 Ibid.

5 Ibid. U.S. teens ages 13–18, n=1,490, Nov. 4–16. 2016. U.S. adults 19 and older, n=1,517, Nov. 4–16, 2016.

Chapter Three

EVERYONE HAS A RELIGION

My second point is:

> 2. There is no non-religious position.

Everyone has a worldview through which they view the world. That worldview is based on beliefs (presuppositions) people have about who they are, where the universe and life came from, how they should live, etc. A worldview doesn't just come from out of nowhere. It is founded in the beliefs people have about their existence and reality. Everyone has beliefs. For instance, if someone rejects God and believes life and the universe came into existence by natural processes, then that is their religion. A religion doesn't mean someone believes in a god of some sort. One of the definitions of religion from the Merriam-Webster online dictionary is:

> *a cause, principle, or system of beliefs held to with ardor and faith.*

That definition encompasses atheism. And remember from the previous chapter, the Bible makes it clear there is no neutral position. This means everyone has a religion. There's no "non-religious" position. In the next chapter I will explain why ultimately there are only two religions (God's Word or man's word), which fits with what the Bible teaches us about two foundations (rock or sand) and two roads (broad way and narrow way).

Because of a lack of teaching, many people just don't understand there's no neutrality and that there is no non-religious position. As a result, they don't understand that when the Bible and prayer were removed from public schools, it didn't make schools neutral. When the Bible, prayer, creation, etc., were by and large removed from the public education system, it was claimed that religion was removed. But in reality, Christianity was removed and replaced with the religion of secular humanism — of atheism.

Christians need to come to grips with the fact that public schools today are brainwashing their children for hours a day in an anti-God religion. I suggest this has greatly contributed to the large numbers of the younger generations leaving the church. And, sadly, many church leaders have given the people in their congregation assurance that sending them to this secular system basically unarmed for the spiritual battle was "okay." In chapters five and six I will detail how we need to be training the younger generations so they can be prepared to do battle against the forces of secular humanism and deal with the spiritual battle raging around us.

This lack of understanding in regard to the fact that there is no neutrality and everyone (or every system) is religious has also contributed to many not battling the moral issues in the right way. We will see how we should be doing this battle in chapter six. Also, many have been bullied into thinking that when atheist groups get nativity scenes, crosses, prayer, Christmas carols, and any reminder of Christianity removed from schools, public places, shopping centers, etc., they are allowing religion to be removed so the places can be neutral. But, in reality, what has happened is that atheists have removed Christian reminders and thus forced their atheism on people.

Because of our history, in the USA (and the rest of the Western world), there was, to one degree or another, a veneer of Christianity in the culture. Even in the public school system the Bible was allowed to be used, students were taught about a creationist viewpoint, and prayer was allowed at assemblies and football games, etc. My point is that the older generations had a public education system that was to one degree or another "Christianized." There was little antagonism toward Christianity. But that has all changed. Progressively over the years, as the culture became more secularized, the schools began shedding reminders of Christianity. Today this secular system is quite atheistic and antagonistic to the Christian worldview. The younger generations have grown up in a much more secularized, anti-God environment than the older generations. Sadly, many in the older generations don't really understand this because of the misunderstanding as to what is a "religion" and that neutrality doesn't exist.

Now, the older generations — the boomers, the silent, and the greatest — grew up in a more Christianized America, with more of a Judeo-Christian ethic based on the Bible. This was because most of the founding fathers of America built their worldview from God's Word, even if they weren't born again (true Christians). The Bible and Christian principles had a great influence on their thinking, which makes sense, as one of the primary reasons they came to America was for religious freedom. So they had a more Christianized morality. Similarly, even if many in the generations of the early-to-mid-twentieth century (greatest, silent, boomers) were not Christian, they still were very Christianized in their thinking. In other words, to them, marriage is between a man and a woman, abortion and homosexual behavior were wrong, etc. They had a morality that largely fit with a morality based on God's Word. Actually, this Christianized worldview permeated the Western world. But when you look at the younger generations — Generation X, the millennials, and then Generation Z — they are the more secularized — more atheistic. These younger generations grew up and are growing up in a much more (and becoming progressively more so at a very rapid pace) secularized atheistic education system. The religion of atheism has greatly impacted them. Even though many of them were brought up in church, many have walked out of church because the secular worldview they were indoctrinated in obviously contradicted a clear reading of the Bible.

Now, we're seeing a consequence of these younger generations building a whole different worldview, which is really an outworking of a more atheistic religious system. Now as these younger generations become the dominant voting bloc in a nation, they will catastrophically change the culture from the more Christianized one of the past to a more secularized one based on autonomous man determining truth. This is happening before our eyes in America and the rest of the Western world. It's happening in the USA, United Kingdom, Canada, New Zealand, and Australia. In England, church attendance is down to around 4%, but it was much greater in the past. We've been losing the younger generations from the church for many years.

Anything Goes

Why are we losing those generations? And why are we losing the culture from a Christian perspective? In America, the culture is becoming less Christianized every day. But this is happening across the whole Western world. In fact, you could describe our culture like the description given in the Book of Judges:

> *In those days there was no king in Israel. Everyone did what was right in his own eyes* (Judges 21:25).

When people ask me, "What has happened to the culture?" I explain it in summary this way:

> *If you raise up generations to believe that the Bible is not true, that the Bible is not the foundation for your thinking, and if you send them to the present increasingly very secular, anti-God education system, let them be indoctrinated through the anti-God secular media so they're brainwashed into thinking it is man who determines truth, then ultimately anything goes.*

I assert that this has been happening to the younger generations for years, and now we're seeing the resulting moral relativism permeate the culture. I grew up in Australia, which is a fairly pagan country. When I was a teenager in high school, the moral issues confronting us today, such as gay "marriage," abortion, pedophilia, racism, gender, euthanasia, etc. weren't major issues. But they certainly are major issues today throughout the entire Western world! Now here we are as Christians, raising up children and grandchildren at this time when there's a tornado of moral relativism ripping through the culture. And we ask, "How do I stop my kids or my grandkids from being swept away by this moral relativism tornado? How can I stop them from being *tossed to and fro by waves and carried about by every wind of doctrine, by human cunning, by craftiness in deceitful schemes?*" (Ephesians 4:14).

So that we may no longer be children, tossed to and fro by the waves and carried about by every wind of doctrine, by human cunning, by craftiness in deceitful schemes. (Ephesians 4:14, ESV)

My wife and I have 5 kids and 18 grandchildren. My wife often says to me, "I'm scared about the culture our grandkids are growing up in."

So, what can we do? Well, first of all, we need to understand what happened.

What Should We Do?

Pastors and parents: Start teaching kids foundationally. We often treat the Bible like a guidebook to life or a collection of moral teachings. But that is a shallow view of God's Word. It is the inspired, infallible, authoritative Word from our Creator that forms the basis for a truly Christian worldview. We need to be teaching our congregations and families from that perspective.

Pastors: Do what you can to get families, including children and young people, reading their Bibles! We have a generation of biblically illiterate adults and young people. Encourage them to get into God's Word individually and as a family.

Parents (particularly fathers!): Lead your family in daily worship time where you read the Bible together; sing good, theologically solid songs (the best of the old and the new); and pray together.

Pastors and parents: Teach children and young people the truth of God's Word and answers to the common questions of our day from a young age — it's never too early to start (but also keep in mind it's never too late to start either!).

Chapter Four

ONLY TWO
RELIGIONS

My third point is:

    3. There are ultimately only two religions — two foundations for our worldview.

What Happened?

The Bible tells us what happened. What happened began in a Garden six thousand years ago when God came to the first man, Adam, and said, "Adam, you can eat of all trees, but there is one tree you're not to eat of, because if you do, you'll surely die." In other words, "Adam, obey God's word."

We know what happened. The devil came to Eve in the form of a serpent, asking (in Genesis 3:1), *"Did God actually say …?"* I want you to notice something.

The first attack was on the authority of the Word of God. *Don't believe God's Word. Doubt God's Word. Did God really say?* The devil was advocating that Adam and Eve reject God's Word and trust their own word. This was the beginning of a battle that has raged unabated for 6,000 years. It's a battle between God's Word and man's word:

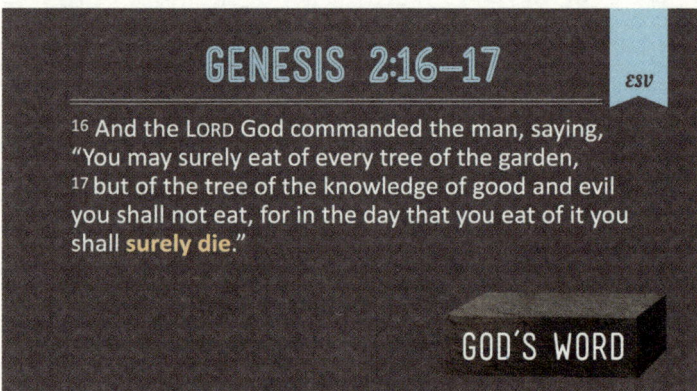

GENESIS 2:16–17

ESV

¹⁶ And the Lord God commanded the man, saying, "You may surely eat of every tree of the garden, ¹⁷ but of the tree of the knowledge of good and evil you shall not eat, for in the day that you eat of it you shall **surely die**."

GOD'S WORD

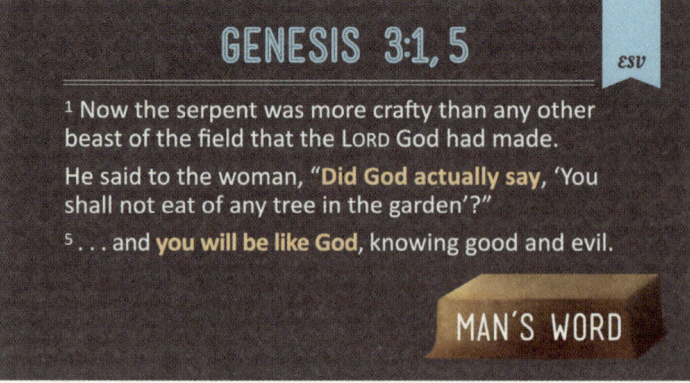

GENESIS 3:1, 5

ESV

¹ Now the serpent was more crafty than any other beast of the field that the Lord God had made.

He said to the woman, "**Did God actually say**, 'You shall not eat of any tree in the garden'?"

⁵ . . . and **you will be like God**, knowing good and evil.

MAN'S WORD

Did God Actually Say?

Let's look at 2 Corinthians 11:3:

> *But I am afraid that as the serpent deceived Eve by his cunning, your thoughts will be led astray from a sincere and pure devotion to Christ.*

Here God, through the Apostle Paul, has a warning for us. He is warning us that the devil is going to use the same method on us, on our kids, on our grandkids, as he did on Eve, to get us all to a position of not believing the things of God. Now what was the method he used on Eve? The devil asked, *"Did God actually say ...?"* He creates doubt regarding trusting the very clear Word of God. Doubt can put people on a slippery slide leading to unbelief. I call this method "the Genesis 3 attack." There's been a Genesis 3 attack ever since the Garden, but it manifests itself in different ways in different eras.

For instance, were Peter and Paul asked questions about carbon dating? No, that wasn't an issue in their day. Do you think Martin Luther was asked if dinosaurs went on the Ark? No. The word "dinosaur" wasn't even invented until 1841. But they did get asked all sorts of questions, and there were attacks on God's Word. People have had to deal with all sorts of attacks on God's Word down through the ages. We need to be asking ourselves, "What's the Genesis 3 attack today?"

If we are going to be raising children or teaching adults, young people, or children in our churches, Sunday schools, colleges, etc., we need to know that the Genesis 3 attack is in our day. God has warned us that the devil will use such an attack to try to take people away from God's Word. We need to make sure that as part of our teaching, we are equipping all ages to be ready to deal with this attack.

Now, think back to that list of questions I gave in Chapter 2:

Don't we live in a scientific age?
Hasn't science disproved the Bible?
How do you know the Bible is true?
What evidence is there for God?
If there is a God, who made God?
*You believe in Adam and Eve? Well, where did
    Cain get his wife?*
*How did the races come about if there were only
    two people to start with?*
Where's the evidence of Noah's Flood?
*Don't fossil layers prove millions of years in
    evolution?*
*We know man evolved from apelike creatures, so
    how could the story of Adam and Eve be true?*
*How can you believe in a loving God with all the
    death and suffering we see in the world?*

> *Didn't dinosaurs live millions of years ago and
>   evolve into birds?*
> *How could Noah fit all the animals on the Ark?*
> *Hasn't science proved evolution is true?*
> *Isn't the Bible an outdated book of mythology?*
> *Don't Muslims and Christians believe in the same
>   God?*
> *What's wrong with gay "marriage" if two people love
>   each other?*

Most of these questions pertain to what's happening in our culture today. And because of the worldwide impact of evolutionary ideas, these questions mostly relate to the Book of Genesis. In our day, there's been an incredible attack on Genesis 1–11 in particular. And this has caused great doubt leading to unbelief in the younger generations, resulting in many walking away from the church. This has also greatly weakened the church's impact on the younger generations and subsequently the culture as a whole.

This attack on Genesis is today's Genesis 3 attack. And because so many of our church leaders and families didn't give answers (teach apologetics) to the younger generations, this has greatly weakened the church's impact generationally and on the culture. Sadly, many church leaders, Christian college professors, etc. compromised God's Word with evolutionary ideas. This has been destructive to people standing on the authority of the Word of God. Such compromise undermines the authority of God's Word, allowing that doubt to lead to unbelief.

A Battle Between Two Religions

Now the battle itself, this battle over authority, is nothing new. As I said, it began in a Garden six thousand years ago. Really, it's a battle between two religions: God's Word and man's word. These are the two starting points for building our worldview.

MAN'S WORD   GOD'S WORD

Many people have the false idea that there are hundreds of religions. In an ultimate sense, there are actually only two: God's Word and man's word.

What about people who take man's ideas in regard to evolution and millions of years and add these to God's Word and reinterpret what it states to fit these ideas in?

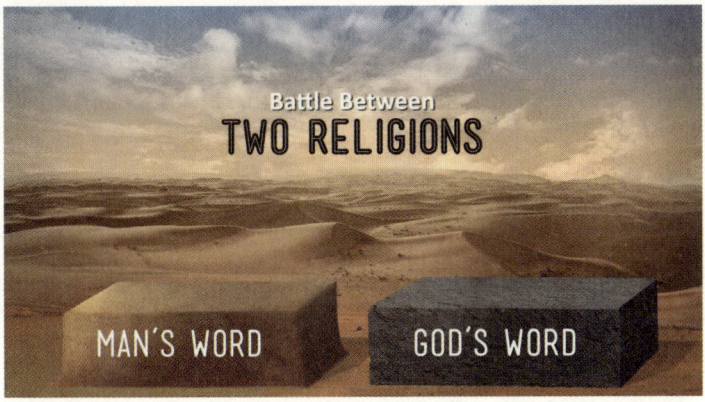

It's vital to understand that when you add man's fallible ideas into God's Word, your starting point is no longer God's Word, it's man's word. Once you introduce man's fallible ideas into God's Word, you no longer have a starting point based entirely in what the infinite Creator God, who knows all things, has revealed to us.

Do we really understand what the Bible is? Do we understand that this means that this is God's Word? As I've traveled all over the world, including speaking in hundreds of churches of different denominations here in the United States, for the past 40 years, I get a bit of a snapshot of the church that most people never see. Really, I've experienced a "bird's-eye view" of the trends and patterns in the Western church.

I've certainly heard many Christian leaders bemoan the trend of losing the younger generations from the church as we've been discussing. In this book I'm detailing where I believe many have failed in correctly dealing with the situation. I'm also particularly addressing five areas that I believe need immediate attention in homes and churches: *Understanding there is no neutral position; understanding there is no non-religious position; understanding there are ultimately only two religions — two foundations for our worldview (the subject of this chapter); equipping people with general Bible and creation apologetics; and understanding how to think foundationally to develop a truly Christian worldview.*

Music — The Way to Keep People Attending?

Instead of dealing with the fundamental foundational issue at the heart of this problem, I have seen a trend in much of the modern church to attempt to attract people to the church and keep the younger generations in church. I digress for a bit now to deal with this. The topic is music.

Now I know this can be a very emotional topic, and I don't want people to misunderstand me. I love music and love to sing great worship hymns and songs. But let me explain what I have observed and experienced.

Music seems to have become a very dominant part of many church services and programs. I personally believe one of the reasons music has become such a dominant feature in the church is that church leaders recognize they are losing coming generations and that the church is not impacting the culture as it used to. So they think more music and performance will attract these younger generations back to church. But based on my experience and the research we've conducted, I believe the church needs in-depth, relevant teaching on topics such as creation and Bible apologetics to answer skeptical questions and equip people to defend the faith.

Now, don't get me wrong! As I've stated above, I love music. In our younger years, my wife, Mally, and I often played piano and organ together in church. And sometimes Steve Hess and Southern Salvation — our resident singing group at the Ark Encounter — talk me into playing piano with them.

So I'm not against music! But I am alarmed by the consistent trends I've observed in a majority of churches. I recognize that what we like or dislike regarding music can be very subjective. But here is my personal philosophy of church music, based on my years of teaching in churches across the world and talking to people and listening to their feedback.

Mix the best of the old with a balance of the new. On rare occasions, when the worship leader sings a classic hymn, I notice that people really sing, though often the young musicians have a hard time playing along since they're not used to such music. Many churches have a contemporary service and a traditional service. So that really divides the church with the older generations usually attending the traditional service and the younger generation attending the contemporary service. A blend of classic hymns with new worship songs could allow everyone to worship together.

Use songs suitable for congregational singing. I've noticed that praise and worship teams, in most instances, have become performance oriented with flashing lights and a nightclub atmosphere. Many of the songs they sing aren't really suitable for congregational singing. Often while the team performs on stage, hardly anyone around me is singing. Performance songs (either from a group, solo, or choir) can be great, but worship leaders should recognize when a song is meant for performance.

Whether in classic hymns or more contemporary songs, check the lyrics against God's Word to make sure they're theologically correct — and make sure people will know what the words of the song mean. If you analyze many of the songs sung in churches today, you will find one or a combination of these problems: They're shallow, theologically incorrect, or unclear in what message they're supposedly conveying.

Be sensitive to the fact that not all people can stand for long periods of time — let people know they don't have to stand. I have a chronic back problem, so for me (and others like me), standing for long periods in one place is difficult. Many elderly people also cannot stand for long periods. It's hard to focus on the teaching when your body is aching from standing so long during the singing portion of the service.

Have at least equal time between the music and the teaching of the Word. Actually, I believe the teaching of the Word should be seen as the priority. As I've talked to people, I find (and surveys have confirmed) that people mainly want good teaching to nurture and equip them. Music has become the dominant part of church services to the detriment of in-depth Bible teaching. What many churches call their praise and worship time becomes the main part of the service, often lasting for 45 minutes to an hour, with only 20–30 minutes of teaching.

The bottom line is this: In all we do, we must make sure we are glorifying God, not man. Our church services should edify believers so they will be equipped in the Word to defend the Christian faith and be powerful witnesses for the Lord Jesus Christ.

What's happened, I believe, is we're not dealing with the foundational reason as to why we're really losing these young people. Sadly, increased entertainment with an emphasis on music becomes the main feature in many instances, with the teaching of the Word watered down and/or relegated to a very short space of time. But people need to be taught how to defend the faith. They need to understand what they believe and why, and how to effectively communicate God's Word and the gospel to someone who has the foundation of man's word. They need to understand how a Christian should be thinking and how a secular person thinks. They need to understand what it means to have a truly Christian worldview and how they can challenge those with a secular worldview.

My point is, music is great, but it's not the answer to the fundamental problems of our age in enabling Christians to raise up godly generations and impact the culture for the Lord Jesus Christ.

What Actually Is the Bible?

Another snapshot of the church involves how lots of people actually view the Bible.

Do we know what the Bible actually is? It is a revelation from God, who knows everything there is to know about everything, who has revealed to us the elements of history that we need to understand so we can build the right worldview to understand this world. Consider these verses of Scripture:

> *And we also thank God constantly for this, that when you received the word of God, which you heard from us, you accepted it not as the word of men but as what it really is, the word of God, which is at work in you believers* (1 Thessalonians 2:13).

> *All Scripture is breathed out by God and profitable for teaching, for reproof, for correction, and*

for training in righteousness, that the man of God may be complete, equipped for every good work (2 Timothy 3:16–17).

But he answered, "It is written, 'Man shall not live by bread alone, but by every word that comes from the mouth of God' " (Matthew 4:4).

Every word of God proves true; he is a shield to those who take refuge in him. Do not add to his words, lest he rebuke you and you be found a liar (Proverbs 30:5–6).

Everyone then who hears these words of mine and does them will be like a wise man who built his house on the rock (Matthew 7:24).

The sum of your word is truth, and every one of your righteous rules endures forever (Psalm 119:160).

Forever, O LORD, your word is firmly fixed in the heavens (Psalm 119:89).

Sadly, during my extensive travels speaking to Christians, I've found a lot of people seem to look on the Bible as mainly a book of spiritual things, moral things, and relationships. To many, it's sort of a guidebook to life that you add to your thinking. But if we truly understood what the Bible is, we would know that this is a revelation from the One who is infinite in knowledge and wisdom. And this is the foundation for all our thinking.

Remember, in Christ are hidden *all the treasures of wisdom and knowledge* (Colossians 2:3). We need to understand that the Bible is not just a guidebook for life, it is the revelation that should be foundational to our worldview.

How Could a Loving God. . . ?

Let me explain what I mean with a practical example.

We're living in this world, and we live in the present. Now one of the most-asked questions from millennials, based on our research and experience, is, "How can there be a loving God with all the death and suffering in the world?"

How do we answer that, as it's true that it's a fairly ugly world with all the death, suffering, and disease that permeates it? We need to start with the foundation of God's Word beginning in Genesis. God's Word tells us it was a perfect world, but man sinned, and death, disease, and suffering are a consequence of man's rebellion. As Romans 8:22–23 states, *For we know that the whole creation has been groaning together in the pains of childbirth until now. And not only the creation, but we ourselves, who have the firstfruits of the Spirit, groan inwardly as we wait eagerly for adoption as sons, the redemption of our bodies.*

Everyone needs to understand that the world we now live in is not the world as God originally made it. This is a fallen world because of our sin. If we don't start with that foundation of God's Word in Genesis, we will not be able to understand this world correctly. In other words, we must start from God's Word to build a truly Christian worldview. If we don't start from God's Word and build a truly Christian worldview, there is only one other foundation (or starting point), and that's man's word, which builds a whole different worldview, a secular one.

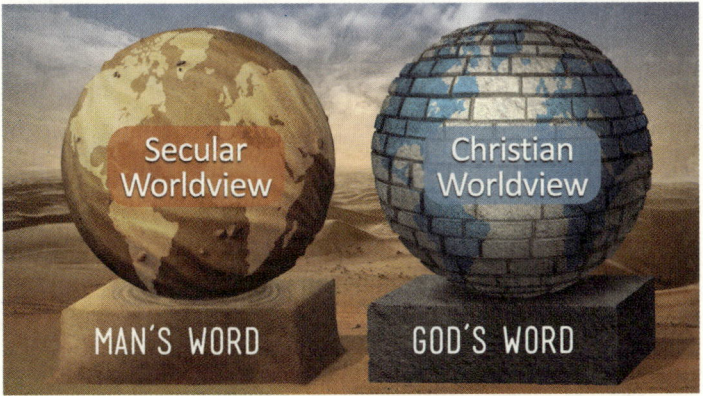

Let me illustrate how this problem about understanding death, disease, and suffering plays out in our families and churches. Atheists claim there can't be a God of love because of all the horrible things we see happening in our world. So, through the media and secular education system, students will be brainwashed to think that if they believe in God, He must be an ogre because of all the awful things that happen. So they begin to question whether there can be a loving God. Now if they attend a church where leaders have compromised the idea of millions of years with the Bible, these children and young people will be told that all the death and suffering they observe has gone on for millions of years. Not only that, but in many of their study materials (Sunday school lessons/Bible studies) and books, they will be told that God created this beautiful world we live in. In many Christian books for young children, they will read that God created all the things we see around us today. But that's a major problem! When you look at the world around us, it is full of death, disease, and suffering. Thus, it is reinforced to these students that God can't be a God of love if He created all these awful things. But if parents and church leaders teach these students to build their thinking on God's Word beginning in Genesis, they will then develop a right way of thinking about this present world. This world is not as God made it. When God made everything, it was very good. But now, because of man's sin, it is a groaning world. The death, disease, and suffering is a result of our sin — it's our fault. But God stepped into history in the person of Jesus Christ to rescue us from the mess we caused. We must teach the coming generation to develop a truly Christian world-view founded in God's Word.

One of the things that burdens me as I've spoken across this nation to Christian school groups is that many of these Christian schools use primarily secular text-books. They try to add God and Christian teaching to those textbooks. But if we correctly understand there's no neutrality and that our thinking as Christians must have the foundation of God's Word, not man's word, then we realize we can't Christianize something that has the wrong foundation. It is not going to work. It's either Christian or secular. Now one can, in a sense, Christianize a way of thinking, but when contaminating God's Word with man's beliefs, ultimately such contamination destroys.

You are the salt of the earth, but if salt has lost its taste, how shall its saltiness be restored? It is no longer good for anything except to be thrown out and trampled under people's feet (Matthew 5:13). Contamination destroys. And such contamination is rife through much of the church, and it has weakened the impact of the church, which is why so many Christian institutions today could be described like the Laodicean church in Revelation 3:15–16, *I know your works: you are neither cold nor hot. Would that you were either cold or hot! So, because you are lukewarm, and neither hot nor cold, I will spit you out of my mouth.* Now that's another warning for churches who are like this.

A Worldview Consistent with a Foundation

Let me now give you a big picture perspective of what I believe has caused so many in the younger generations to walk away from the church. Statistics in the USA indicate that over 90% of kids from church homes attend public schools for their education. However, many in the older generations don't realize how atheistic and antagonistic to Christianity this system has become. The older generations (particularly the greatest, silent, and baby boomers) went to the public education system when it was much more Christianized. For instance, the Bible was allowed to be read, prayer at various times was allowed, Christmas carols were sung at Christmas time with nativity scenes allowed in school, teachers could teach about creation in the classes, etc.

But the situation has dramatically changed for the X, Y, and Z generations. The secular education system, as discussed previously, has basically thrown any reminders of Christian thinking out, and now students are taught that the whole of reality is explained by natural processes. The supernatural is not allowed. Also, increasingly we see the leftist social agenda playing out as kids are subjected to indoctrination to accept the LGBTQ+ worldview, abortion, critical race theory, man-caused climate change, atheistic evolution, and more.

The students from church homes then come to our churches with the foundation the education system has taught them for their worldview, that "it's man who determines truth and God has nothing to do with knowledge." But, in many instances, instead of church leaders and parents teaching these students the foundation of God's Word to develop a truly Christian worldview beginning in Genesis, those teaching them try to impose a Christian worldview on their current thinking. It won't work because they have the wrong foundation of man's word. So ultimately, any Christian thinking imposed on them eventually collapses.

Eventually these students then build a worldview consistent with the foundation they have.

And as they leave the church, they become much more secular and atheistic, consistent with the foundation that they were taught to have. We see this particularly in Generation Z, who researcher George Barna found were twice as atheistic as any previous generation.

Whose Fault Is It?

So, whose fault is it that this situation has occurred? I believe it's the fault of families and much of the church because they didn't raise up generations with the right foundation to have the right worldview, knowing what they believe and why, and being equipped with answers to defend the Christian worldview against attacks from the world. So, what can we do?

I've already stated there are five main items churches and families need to take heed of and begin implementing.

I've already dealt with the first three: *There is no neutral position; there is no non-religious position; and there are ultimately only two religions — two foundations for our worldview.*

Now I want to deal with the last two: *General Bible and creation apologetics, and how to think foundationally to develop a truly Christian worldview.*

What Can We Do?

Pastors: Carefully and prayerfully consider how you're approaching the mass exodus of young people from the church. Are you trying to entertain them so they stick around? Or are you giving them what they truly need — rich teaching, starting with God's Word as the foundation, that counters the sand of the teaching of the world and helps them have the correct foundation to build a truly Christian worldview on?

Give answers to your congregations. Practice working apologetics into your sermons.

Chapter Five

READY TO GIVE AN ANSWER

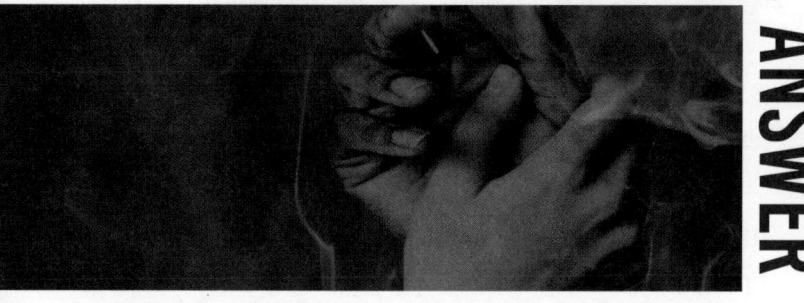

My fourth point is:

    4. General Bible and creation apologetics.

Many churches and homes have failed to teach apologetics to all ages in their congregations and families.

What do I mean by apologetics? The word "apologetics" comes from the Greek word transliterated *apologia* as used in 1 Peter 3:15. Greek lexicons give that meaning as *a verbal defense, speech in defense; a reasoned statement or argument.*

> *But in your hearts honor Christ the Lord as holy, always being prepared to make a defense to anyone who asks you for a reason for the hope that is in you; yet do it with gentleness and respect* (1 Peter 3:15).

The King James Version uses the word "answer" instead of defense:

> But sanctify the Lord God in your hearts: and be ready always to give an answer to every man that asketh you a reason of the hope that is in you with meekness and fear (1 Peter 3:15).

The word *apologia* means to "speak away" the accusation. In other words, to give a logical, reasoned defense of one's position.

I believe there has been a great lack of teaching of apologetics in our homes and churches. Think back to the sampling of those typical questions I said people ask today. As you read them again, be asking yourself: How would I answer them? Can I answer them? Have I taught my children or my classes in church and/or the congregation how to answer them? How many people in my church or home could answer them? Here they are again:

> Don't we live in a scientific age?
> Hasn't science disproved the Bible?
> How do you know the Bible is true?
> What evidence is there for God?
> If there is a God, who made God?
> You believe in Adam and Eve? Well, where did Cain get his wife?

*How did the races come about if there were only two
people to start with?*

Where's the evidence of Noah's Flood?

*Don't fossil layers prove millions of years in
evolution?*

*We know man evolved from apelike creatures, so
how could the story of Adam and Eve be true?*

*How can you believe in a loving God with all the
death and suffering we see in the world?*

*Didn't dinosaurs live millions of years ago and
evolve into birds?*

How could Noah fit all the animals on the Ark?

Hasn't science proved evolution is true?

Isn't the Bible an outdated book of mythology?

*Don't Muslims and Christians believe in the same
God?*

*What's wrong with gay "marriage" if two people love
each other?*

No matter what country I'm in or whatever size of audience (from hundreds to thousands), whenever I ask the audience to put their hands up if they have heard those sorts of questions today, nearly all the hands go up every time. Now that wouldn't have happened in Peter and Paul's day or Luther's day, as they had to deal with mostly different sorts of questions. But those questions are true of what most people have heard of today. Why is it?

Can We Answer These Questions?

It's because those questions relate to the Genesis 3 attack of our day. Remember, Paul warned us that the devil would use the same method on us as he did on Eve to get us to not believe God's Word. That's the devil's method. The method has never changed, but the way the method manifests itself does change as represented in the types of attacks on God's Word down through the ages. The whole world today is permeated with the teaching of evolution and millions of years that has resulted in these sorts of questions being asked. And if we can't answer them, they can begin to cause doubt in regard to God's Word, and that doubt can ultimately lead to unbelief. When I'm speaking to audiences, I always notice that when I ask the following questions, it's like a deathly silence spills across the audience:

> *How many of us can really answer those questions adequately right now? How many of us have taught our children and young people the answers to those questions? How many of us have taught our Sunday schools, youth groups, Bible studies, and congregations we minister to the answers to them?*

By and large, what I found in the church in America (and other places in the West) is there's an emphasis on teaching the good news of the gospel in the sense of the death and Resurrection of Jesus and our need for salvation (which is all grounded in Genesis!). Also, I find there's often significant teaching on Revelation and end times. But how much teaching is there on Genesis and specifically Genesis 1–11? Not that much. I've even experienced some conservative pastors tell me it is too controversial for them to teach Genesis 1–11 because some people in the church believe in evolution and millions of years, so it would create division within their church. Because they want to avoid division, they avoid teaching Genesis except in a very general sense. But Genesis 1–11 is the foundation for the whole Bible, for all our doctrine, and for our Christian worldview. Actually, because much of the church hasn't taught the literal history of Genesis 1–11, I submit it's a major reason many of the younger generations have left the church and why the culture has become so secularized. I will explain this more fully when we deal with what it means to teach the right foundation beginning with Genesis for our Christian worldview.

I believe we need a new Reformation to get God's people (the church) back to the authority of the Word of God beginning in Genesis. I also believe many parents and Christian leaders need to repent of not raising up generations to think foundationally and be equipped with answers to defend the Christian faith. Many need to repent of compromising God's Word with man's fallible ideas of evolution and millions of years.

The 7 C's of History

When you visit the two leading Christian-themed attractions in the world, the Ark Encounter and Creation Museum, you will find we have an emphasis on teaching apologetics (giving answers to the skeptical questions leveled at God's Word) and teaching foundationally (helping people build a truly Christian worldview to correctly understand life and the universe).

A centerpiece of all our exhibits at the Creation Museum is the walk through the Bible that we call "The 7 C's of History."

It was always my burden to have this at the Creation Museum — a walk through the Bible, which is really walking through the history of the universe, life, and this world that God has revealed to us.

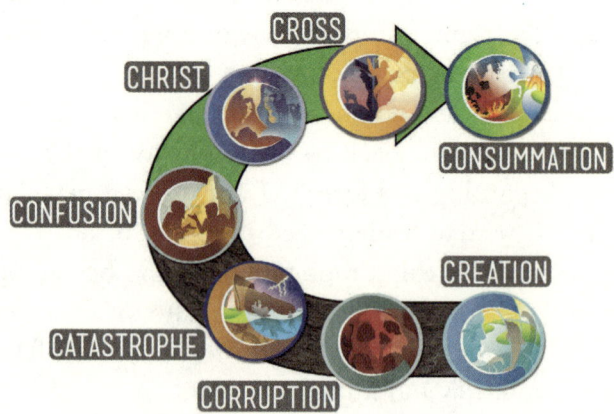

As people walk through the 7 C's, they experience a walk through the major events of history that God has revealed to us so that we will have the right foundation to build a right worldview to correctly understand the world, the purpose and meaning of life, salvation, and more.

In summary, this history consists of:

Creation: A perfect creation.

Corruption: Sin and death enter the world because of our sin in Adam. God promises a Savior.

Catastrophe: The Flood of Noah's day, which lays down fossils all over the world. Noah's Ark with its one door is a picture of Jesus — a picture of salvation.

Confusion: God confuses the language of the post-Flood population, resulting in people moving out over the earth and forming different cultures and nations.

Christ: God's Son steps into history as the Godman to fulfill the promise of the Savior.

Cross: Jesus Christ dies on the Cross and rises from the dead so those who receive the free gift of salvation will be saved and will live with the Lord forever in heaven when they die.

Consummation: One day, Jesus will bodily return to earth and judge the present creation with fire and make a new heavens and earth.

Biblical Glasses — The Right Prescription

The first four C's are actually the geological, biological, astronomical, and anthropological history that God gives us. Think of those four C's as a pair of glasses.

We all need to wear these glasses 24 hours a day so that we are always looking at the world through them. We need to raise our children to put on these glasses basically from when they are born. As they look through these glasses,

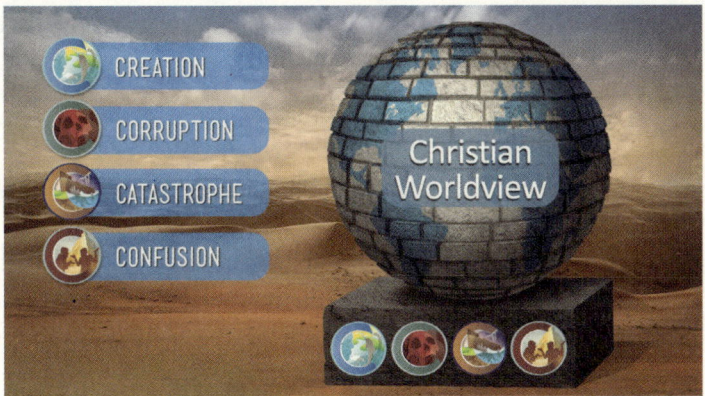

then they understand: Why there is so much death, suffering and disease? Because of our sin. Why there are fossils all over the world? Because of Noah's Flood. Why there are many different cultures but only one race of people? Because of the Tower of Babel event. Why do we need a Savior? Because of our sin in Adam. Why does everything exist? Because God created an originally perfect creation.

And the history those four C's represent are foundational to the rest of the Bible, to all doctrine, to our Christian worldview, and to the gospel.

Where are we in history? We are between the last two C's. Look at the 7 C's again and think about the fact that all that's represented by the first 6 C's has already happened. We are now waiting for the events of the 7th C. And the way things are in our culture, the more we want to see the 7th C happen!

But I have to tell you that even that could be another 1,000 years away! (Sorry to disappoint you.) Then again, it could be in 100 years' time. Or it could be tomorrow! We just don't know the date when Jesus will return. Certainly, the Bible tells us of signs to look for. But I suggest instead of focusing on when we think the Lord's return will be, we should be focusing on what Jesus taught us in the parable in Luke 19. Let's read through the first part of that parable:

> *He said therefore, "A nobleman went into a far country to receive for himself a kingdom and then return. Calling ten of his servants, he gave them ten minas, and said to them, 'Engage in business until I come'"* (Luke 19:12–13).

Although some scholars have some differing ways of interpreting this parable, I believe it can be applied this way. The nobleman represents Jesus; the servants represent us (Christians). Jesus entrusts resources to people. Now these resources could be material, such as finances. But they could also be talents such as teaching, speaking, singing, etc. So Jesus entrusts resources to each one of us. Then Jesus says He is going away (His ascension to heaven) and that He will return (the Second Coming). Jesus then says, *Engage in business until I come.*

The sense of *engage in business* is to use the resources to gain a profit. Or we could say to use our resources to do what we can to reap a harvest of souls.

We could put it this way: Our focus should be on doing all we can to proclaim the truth of God's Word and the gospel, regardless of what is happening in the culture, until the Lord returns.

Because we see our Western world collapsing from a Christian worldview perspective, with increasing moral relativism and antagonism to Christianity, I've met Christians who claim that this is a sign the Lord is returning soon, so there's not much point in us doing anything. Basically, we just need to get ready, as the end is nigh!

But we don't know where we are in history. And things may look bad in our culture, but there are places around the world where the church is increasing in its impact. Maybe the West will collapse and then a new Reformation will bring revival, and things will dramatically change. We don't know.

Other Christians have told me they are so depressed because of what is happening, and they don't know what to do. But I insist we do know what to do. We are to engage in the business of the King until He returns. And God's Word instructs us how to do this:

Contend for the faith (Jude 1:3).

Proclaim the gospel (Mark 16:15).

Engage in business of the King of kings till He comes (Luke 19:13).

Equip people with answers (1 Peter 3:15).

Call compromising Christians, church leaders, and academics back to the authority of God's Word, beginning in Genesis, and encourage them to stand boldly for God's Word and to stop being lukewarm (Revelation 3:16).

Help raise up godly generations to be salt and light in the dark world by teaching the next generation the gospel and the Word of God (Matthew 5; Mark 9).

Be a watchman to warn people what is happening (Ezekiel 33:6).

Where Should Our Focus Be?

Before we deal with practical aspects of teaching apologetics and foundations, I want to challenge us concerning another matter.

I have found that many people in the church are fascinated by end times teaching and the Book of Revelation. Often I've seen situations where a church will run a conference dealing with the Book of Revelation, and people will pack the auditorium. Yet if the church runs a conference on Genesis, many claim it's not that important and it's more difficult to get people interested. Many churches will not hesitate to conduct a conference on Revelation but are more reticent to do so on Genesis because they know it will cause some division and/or they don't see it as that important anyway.

Now my challenge!

Revelation is not the foundation for all doctrine. Genesis is. Revelation is not the foundation for a Christian worldview. Genesis is. Revelation is not the foundation for the rest of the Bible. Genesis is. And I maintain it's because of a lack of teaching on Genesis 1–11, combined with the compromise of Genesis 1–11 with evolution and millions of years, that has greatly contributed to a lukewarm church and the devastation of the younger generations in leaving the church. This has also led to the increasing secularization of the culture.

The same problem in regard to a neglect in regard to Genesis 1–11 can be seen in the way many Statements of Faith (or What We Believe) for churches and Christian institutions are written. You will find many of them have more general statements in regard to Genesis (if they mention Genesis at all) but often very specific statements in regard to Revelation or end times. It's obvious in a number of instances that these churches and institutions are more concerned about a particular view of eschatology than they are on taking a stand on the history in Genesis 1–11. And yet, as I said, by not taking the right stand on Genesis 1–11 and teaching that as the foundation for everything, that's a major reason why we have seen the church not impacting the culture as it should.

Because of the Genesis 3 attack today, Christian leaders should understand they need to be very emphatic about details in Genesis 1–11 so it will be effective in stopping compromise with secular ideas. To help us understand this point, I have included the detailed Statement of Faith for the ministry of Answers in Genesis in Appendix 1.

You will see that we have done our best to deal with the current cultural climate in regard to issues that plague us today by being very specific in our wording to try our best to stop people from reinterpreting God's Word. So many churches and Christian institutions have departed from the stand on the authority of God's Word that their founders had because people came into those institutions who had accepted beliefs from the world (like evolution/millions of years, etc.) and thus began to undermine biblical authority. That's why, in regard to Genesis, we have to be specific in the wording in order to not allow such compromise positions. Today we are now seeing some church leaders softening on teaching concerning homosexual behavior, abortion, etc. because of the way the world is now forcing the LGBTQ+ worldview on the culture. We have had to be very specific in our Statement of Faith wording in order to eliminate such people from coming into our organization.

I challenge you all to check out the Statement of Faith (or whatever they call such documents) in your own churches and Christian institutions you support. See how they measure up with what I've written above.

How Many Animals on the Ark?

Now I want to get to a practical example for what we mean by teaching apologetics. In my first year of teaching in Australia in 1975, one of the first questions the students in my science classes asked me went something like this: *Sir, you're a Christian and believe the Bible. But the Bible can't be true. Noah couldn't fit all the animals on the Ark.* As I have traveled for over 40 years around the world speaking, I am asked many of the same questions over and over again. One of the most-asked questions has been about how Noah could fit the animals on the Ark. Atheists will use this question to tell people that it shows the Bible is a myth. For example, when I debated Bill Nye in 2014 at the Creation Museum, he mocked me for believing in Noah's Ark. He said there was no way Noah could fit the millions of species of animals on board. And the way students are taught in public schools about evolution and speciation makes them easy targets for this argument. Many have told me this was a real stumbling block to them.

This is one of the reasons we wanted to build the life-size Noah's Ark attraction, the Ark Encounter. Like we do at the Creation Museum, we wanted to answer many of the most-asked questions that are stumbling blocks to believing the truth of the history in the Bible. At the Ark, we have a number of exhibits that detail how to answer the question about how Noah could fit the animals on the Ark and how many animals were actually needed.

On deck one in the Ark, we have a cutaway model of the Ark. A sign states that (at the most) 1,398 animal kinds were on Noah's Ark. The Bible says God made *kinds* of land animals according to their kind. Notice the Hebrew word (*min*) is not translated as "species" in our Bibles. It's translated as the word "kind." And two of each kind of land-dwelling, air-breathing animal, seven pairs of some, were on board Noah's Ark. (By the way, Spanish Bibles translate the Hebrew word translated "kind" in English versions as "species." But that is not a good or correct translation and creates unfortunate problems).

Look at our man-made classification system: kingdom, phylum, class, order, family, genus, species. Creation scientists say that the Hebrew word *min* is really referring to the *family* level of our classification system. Sometimes it could be at the *order* level, but mostly it would be *family*. For example, if we research dogs, we find they are all classified under one family, *Canidae*.

Dogs Are Dogs

There are around 34 different species of dogs today (e.g., wolves, dingoes, foxes, etc.). Scientists can document they are all interconnected through breeding. If a group of animals are all interconnected in this way, they are considered to be part of the same kind. This means Noah only needed two of the dog kind to go on the Ark. They came off the Ark after the Flood and over time increased in number. Which mates with which, which ones die out, and how they're separated result in different species of dogs forming. This is because of all the genetic diversity God put in the dog kind when He created them. Such speciation is not evolution — they are still dogs in the dog kind. There's been no change of kind, just variation within a kind.

And such speciation can happen quickly because all the genetic information is already present. This helps us understand that Noah didn't take all the species of dogs we observe today, but only two representatives of the dog kind. As we apply this to other animals, we start to realize that Noah didn't need anywhere near the number of animals many people think he did. In fact, our creation scientists think there could be fewer than 1,000 actual kinds of land animals represented on the Ark (1,398 is a "worst-case scenario"). Most land animals are not very large (the average size of a land animal is quite small). There was plenty of room on the Ark for the land animals needed.

In Appendix 2, I have listed some of the basic resources that give answers to the most-asked questions people have today.

Defenseless?

The example above deals with creation apologetics. There are many such questions (like those listed earlier) that come under this category. However, there has also been a great lack of teaching of general Bible apologetics, and this is also vital for people to be equipped with. Most people couldn't answer questions in regard to how the Bible came about, or what it means that it's inspired, or why Christians believe in the Trinity, or why Jesus is God, and so on. Most Christians aren't equipped to be able to answer questions from people in various cults (Jehovah's Witness, Mormon, etc.) or from those involved in Eastern mysticism, etc. I have also featured basic resources to help in this area in Appendix 2.

I believe the lack of teaching of apologetics has helped lead to the high degree of biblical illiteracy in many Christians. Sadly, this causes a problem with the next generation, as parents haven't taught their children how to defend the Christian faith. This makes it easy for the enemy to come and capture defenseless people.

What Should We Do?

Pastors: Teach Genesis, especially chapters 1–11! Many pastors are nervous to teach on this portion of Scripture because so many in their congregation may have strong feelings about issues regarding creation and the age of the earth. But don't be afraid — God honors the faithful teaching of His Word, and this section of Scripture is the foundation to all our doctrine. It's vitally important!

Chapter Six

THINKING

FOUNDATIONALLY

Now we come to the fifth item that has sadly been greatly neglected.

> 5. How to think foundationally to develop a truly Christian worldview.

I assert that, by and large, we haven't raised up generations to think foundationally. What do I mean by that?

How have Christians and church leaders taught their children and congregations to deal with issues like gender; abortion; marriage; and why the world is full of death, disease, and suffering?

Start with the Foundation

How do you build a house? We all know one builds a roof first, then the walls, and then tries to put a foundation underneath.

You would correctly say that doesn't work. You can't build a house from the roof down; it has to be built from the foundation up.

I think many people in our churches have tried to build the Christian structure in our kids using a roof down approach. Think of the Christian worldview, biblical doctrines, and the message of Christ's death and Resurrection (the gospel) as the walls and the roof. Think of the Bible as the foundation. And as I will explain further, Genesis 1–11 is the foundation for the rest of the Bible.

I suggest the way Christianity is often taught is by using the "roof down approach," which assumes the foundation is already there. In reality, that's how many in the older generations in our churches taught the Christian faith. There was an underlying assumption that people had a respect for the Bible and understood to one degree or another it was the Word of God. Thus, the roof and walls of Christianity were taught to people.

The older generations (greatest, silent, and baby boomers) grew up in a Western culture where there was a general respect for the Bible, belief in God, and a general adherence to Christian morality. In other words, one could assume most people had the same basic foundation for much of their thinking.

But that foundation is generally not there for the younger generations (X, Y, Z, and now Alpha). As I stated earlier, there are only two foundations. So if the Bible (God's Word) is not the foundation, the only other is man's word.

To build the structure of Christianity, we have to start with the right foundation, the rock of God's Word. On that foundation we then build the walls and the roof.

If we start with the right foundation, then people will know what they believe, why they believe what they do, and why people who reject Christianity think the way they do. This will also enable a Christian to know how to effectively communicate with non-Christians using a foundational approach. As we will see later, this takes a lot of the emotionalism out of such dialogue and ultimately brings the battle down to the foundational level where it needs to be fought, explaining why the Bible is the only correct foundation.

To know how to respond to the issues of gender, abortion, marriage, death, and suffering, we have to teach people to think foundationally. As we teach foundationally, we also use apologetics as part of teaching how we can defend our positions as Christians.

So how do we deal with these issues listed above? As I discussed earlier, Genesis 1–11 is the foundation for the rest of the Bible, all doctrine, and our Christian worldview. That means when dealing with any issue, the first thing we must do is recognize we have to start with Genesis 1–11. If we don't start there, we won't have the right foundation. We start with the history God has revealed to us that is foundational to all our thinking. We represent this history as the first four C's in the 7 C's of History exhibit at the Creation Museum.

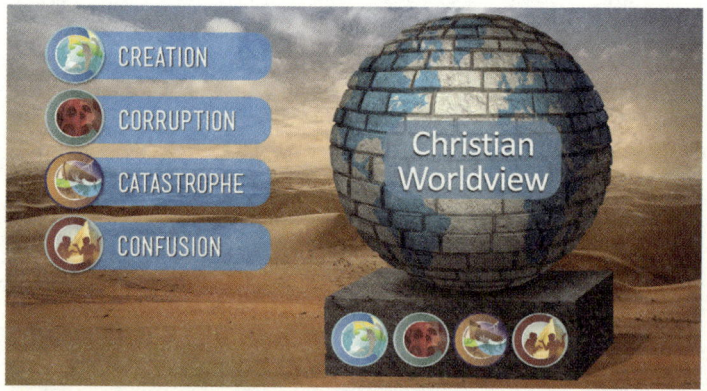

Dealing with Gender

Let's start with Genesis 1–11.

> *So God created man in his own image, in the image of God he created him; male and female he created them* (Genesis 1:27).

When God created the first two humans, we are told He only made two types: male and female. This is attested to throughout the rest of Scripture. For instance:

> *Male and female he created them* (Genesis 5:2).

> *. . . for anyone, male or female* (Leviticus 15:33).

> *Have you not read that he who created them from the beginning made them male and female* (Matthew 19:4).

> *But from the beginning of creation, "God made them male and female"* (Mark 10:6).

When we start with the foundation of God's Word beginning in Genesis 1–11, there are only two genders of humans: male and female. So as Christians, we need to explain to people that because we build our thinking on God's Word, starting with the history in Genesis, our worldview therefore necessitates us understanding there are only two genders in humans. Now we can also use observational science as an argument to confirm this position. This means we also use apologetics to defend what we know to be true based on God's Word.

Human DNA consists of 23 pairs of chromosomes. What are called the sex chromosomes come in two forms: Males have X and Y chromosomes as a pair, while females have X and X.

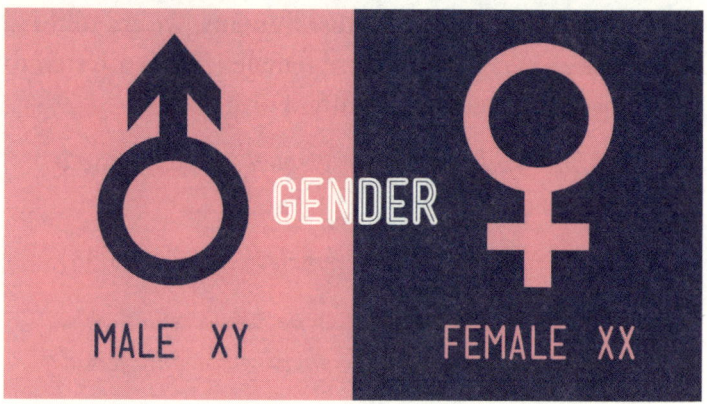

Observational science confirms two genders. However, as part of our understanding, we need to be aware of any objections the world will bring up so we can be prepared to answer them. This needs to be taught to our children (or whoever we are teaching) so they won't be caught off guard.

People will object by saying that there are exceptions to the normal pairing of XY or XX chromosomes. Are there exceptions? Yes, there are, but they are also statistically a very small percentage. For example, some people can have XXX or XXY. How do we explain these (and other) differences? We have to build our thinking on Genesis 1–11. God's Word tells us that God made a perfect creation, but because of our sin, now things run down. Now there are mutations (mistakes) that can occur when genes are copied from one generation to the next. Such mistakes not only happen in the sex chromosomes but happen in other chromosomes as well. Sometimes these mistakes can cause all sorts of problems for those people who have them. But such mistakes do not negate the created order of only two genders in humans, male and female.

Dealing with Abortion

What about the abortion issue? As with any area, to build a Christian worldview, we must start with the foundation of God's Word in Genesis.

> *So God created man in his own image, in the image of God he created him* (Genesis 1:27).

No animals were made in God's image. Only man (Adam and Eve as the first two humans) was made in God's image. God created the animals in a very different way to how he created humans.

For the animals:

> *And God said, "Let the earth bring forth living creatures according to their kinds — livestock and creeping things and beasts of the earth according to their kinds." And it was so* (Genesis 1:24).

For man:

> *Then God said, "Let us make man in our image, after our likeness. And let them have dominion over*

the fish of the sea and over the birds of the heavens and over the livestock and over all the earth and over every creeping thing that creeps on the earth (Genesis 1:26).

Man is obviously different from animals. We are not just specialized animals as the secular world teaches. Kids in most schools are taught that man is in the animal kingdom just like other animals. We are mammals, but we are also made in God's image. So, from a Christian worldview perspective, man should be in a separate section on his own, and not part of the animal kingdom. This would help students realize man is very different from the animals. Man is made in the image of God. This foundational teaching is needed to then enable us to build a Christian worldview in dealing with the issue of abortion.

In sexual reproduction one set of chromosomes (DNA) comes from the mother and one set from the father. DNA from male and female come together at fertilization. So each human being starts as a fertilized egg with DNA from the mother and father.

You know what's interesting about that? This is a unique combination of information, different than the mother, different than the father, but all the information came from both the mother and the father.

When we look at ourselves, we are different from our mother and father, and yet we can see similarities if we have any brothers or sisters. They're different from us and each other, and yet our DNA came from our mother and father. But each person has a unique combination of information.

As the fertilized egg divides to build our body, no new information is ever added.

NO NEW INFORMATION IS ADDED!

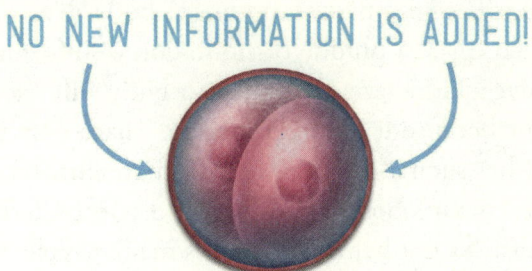

This means each of us are 100% unique. We are each made in God's image right from fertilization. That means abortion at any stage (from the moment of fertilization onward) is killing a human being. As we are made in His image, God's Word clearly teaches we're not to murder another human being. God gave the death penalty for murder in Genesis 9:5–6. Also, as part of the Ten Commandments, we are told, *You shall not murder* (Exodus 20:13).

If man is just an animal, why does it matter if someone murders a human being? If we kill animals, why not kill human beings? But human beings are made in God's image!

Now, what sorts of objections will we hear from the world to justify abortion? Well, here is one of them. We often hear those defending abortion claiming that a woman has a right to do with her body what she wants. How do we answer that? How do we prepare those we teach to know how to deal with such an objection?

Is a fertilized egg part of a woman's body? No, it's not. A fertilized egg is a unique combination of information. If you have a kidney transplant, your body will reject the transplant because it is foreign tissue. That's why someone who has such a transplant has to have anti-rejection drugs. A woman's body actually would reject a fertilized egg because it's not her tissue — it is made of cells with a unique combination of information in the DNA — but God built an anti-rejection mechanism into the uterus so it will accept the fertilized egg and allow it to develop. Simply amazing design by our Creator God.

Also, when someone claims a fertilized egg is part of a woman's body, then consider if the fertilized egg is male with the X and Y sex chromosomes. That can't be part of her body, as the woman's sex chromosomes consist of and X and X.

I was teaching on this topic at the Creation Museum a number of years ago, and a young lady in her late teens came to me after my talk with tears in her eyes. She looked at me and said, "I grew up in the church all my life, and nobody explained to me that it meant that we were made in God's image and we were different from the animals. No one ever explained to me about DNA and the unique combination of information right from fertilization."

And then she looked at me with those tears and said, "What if someone like me has had an abortion?"

I replied to this young lady, telling her that God is a loving God and a forgiving God. I then gave her these Scriptures:

> If we confess our sins, he is faithful and just to forgive us our sins and to cleanse us from all unrighteousness (1 John 1:9).

> As far as the east is from the west, so far does he remove our transgressions from us (Psalm 103:12).

> For I will be merciful toward their iniquities, and I will remember their sins no more (Hebrews 8:12).

After she heard those verses, she had a big smile on her face, said "thank you," and off she went.

At the Creation Museum, we have what I believe is the most powerful pro-life exhibit in the world. It is called *Fearfully and Wonderfully Made*. At the end of this stunning exhibit that deals with all the issues I discussed above and much more, with spectacular models of the development of a child in a mother's womb right from fertilization, we then have teaching about our forgiving God for those who repent of the sin of abortion.

Have you taught your kids foundationally like this? Have pastors equipped their congregations, or Christian college professors equipped their students, foundationally to know how Christians should respond to the abortion issue? Are we preparing people with the right foundation so they will build a truly Christian worldview and know what they believe, why they believe it, and how to defend it?

Dealing with Marriage

Where do we start to know what we should believe in regard to marriage? Genesis 1–11, of course.

Let's consider the main verses of Scripture from Genesis that enable us to have the right foundation to build our Christian worldview regarding marriage.

> *Then the* LORD *God formed the man of dust from the ground and breathed into his nostrils the breath of life, and the man became a living creature* (Genesis 2:7).

> *Then the* LORD *God said, "It is not good that the man should be alone; I will make him a helper fit for him* (Genesis 2:18).

> *The man gave names to all livestock and to the birds of the heavens and to every beast of the field. But for Adam there was not found a helper fit for him* (Genesis 2:20).

> *So the LORD God caused a deep sleep to fall upon the man, and while he slept took one of his ribs and closed up its place with flesh. And the rib that the LORD God had taken from the man he made into a woman and brought her to the man* (Genesis 2:21–22).

Then the man said,

> *"This at last is bone of my bones and flesh of my flesh; she shall be called Woman, because she was taken out of Man"* (Genesis 2:23).

> *Therefore a man shall leave his father and his mother and hold fast to his wife, and they shall become one flesh* (Genesis 2:24).

The Bible tells us that God made man directly from dust. He didn't make him from an ape-man or some previously existing animal. We return to dust when we die (Genesis 3:19), not an ape-man or animal. Evolution does not fit with the Bible's account of the origin of man. And yet, sadly, many Christian leaders believe in evolution and compromise God's Word in Genesis to try to justify that.

Now God said it was not good for the man to be alone. So, He brought animals to Adam to name, to show Adam that no one else was made in the image of God. Then God put Adam to sleep and, from his rib, made the first woman and brought her to Adam.

Note that the woman was made from the man, not from an ape-woman. As Paul states twice in 1 Corinthians, in 11:8 and 11:12, woman came from man, not from an ape-woman or some animal. Again, evolution does not fit with the Bible's account of the creation of humans.

The first recorded words of Adam are when he says Eve is bone of his bones and flesh of his flesh. He called her *woman* because she was taken out of man.

Now Genesis 2:24 tells us God created marriage. Marriage is a God-ordained institution. Marriage was not created by the Supreme Court justices of the United States of America (or anyone else). And when God created marriage, it was one man and one woman, male and female. To teach about marriage, we must start with the foundational history in Genesis. In doing this, we can come to no other conclusion than there is only one type of marriage, the one God ordained in Scripture — one biological male and one biological female.

Do you know who else attests to the historicity of Genesis and the creation of marriage as one man and one woman? Our Creator, the Lord Jesus Christ. Jesus as the

Godman in Matthew 19 (also recorded in Mark 10) was asked about marriage:

> *He answered, "Have you not read that he who created them from the beginning made them male and female, and said, 'Therefore a man shall leave his father and his mother and hold fast to his wife, and the two shall become one flesh'?"* (Matthew 19:4–5).

Note, first of all, Jesus confirms the authority of Scripture (*Have you not read. . .*). He confirms the history in Genesis as literal history and also that there are only two genders of humans (*from the beginning made them male and female*). Jesus then confirms the truth of Genesis 2:24 concerning one flesh, and that in marriage a man leaves his parents and is united with his wife, who is a female. This means there is no such thing as gay "marriage." They can call it a gay union or whatever they want, but it is not marriage. There's only one type of marriage — the one God ordained in Scripture.

By the way, when people want two men or two women in "marriage," why do they many times only want two? Two comes from the Bible based on the true marriage God created in Genesis. Satan always takes what God has done and perverts it as part of his rebellion against his Creator.

The doctrine of marriage is founded in the history in Genesis. That's the foundation for true marriage.

Every Single Doctrine

Now, the history in Genesis is not just foundational to marriage. Ultimately, every single biblical doctrine, directly or indirectly, is founded in Genesis 1–11.

The origin of sin: Genesis 1–11. The origin of death: Genesis 1–11. Why did Jesus die on the Cross? Genesis 1–11. Why is Jesus called the last Adam? Genesis 1–11. Why do humans wear clothes? Genesis 1–11. Why do we

need a new heaven and new earth? Genesis 1–11. Why do we have a seven-day week? Genesis 1–11.

Is Genesis 1–11 important? It's the foundation for all doctrine, the rest of the Bible, and our Christian worldview. And yet, many churches have not taught Genesis this way. Many have compromised Genesis with evolution and millions of years. If generations are raised in our churches and families without the foundation of Genesis 1–11, I submit they will be captured by the world, as has happened. Most kids from the church who go to public schools do not last in the church. Most kids who go to compromising Christian schools, colleges, and seminaries do not last in the church. And many of those who do last end up having a very secular worldview and often support the LGBTQ+ movement, abortion, etc.

Dealing with Death, Suffering, and Disease

How can we believe in a loving God with all the death and suffering in the world? Atheists mock Christians for believing in a loving God because they see an ugly world of death, disease, suffering, and violence.

Where do we start to understand this issue? Genesis 1–11, of course.

And God saw everything that he had made, and behold, it was very good. And there was evening and there was morning, the sixth day (Genesis 1:31).

When God made everything, He said it was *very good*. Today's world is certainly not very good. But here's a problem, as I previously discussed, which I see in many churches. In our churches we often have books or Sunday school materials to teach children that God made this beautiful world. But when kids look at this supposedly beautiful world, they see quite an ugly world. Yes, there is a remnant of beauty, but there is much ugliness in the form of death, various diseases, suffering, violence, and so on.

This is not a beautiful world. It's filled with ugliness because of sin. The original world was beautiful. Here's the problem. If we are not using the foundation of God's Word beginning in Genesis to build a proper Christian worldview, our children will not understand this world they live in. We need to be training these children to put on the Genesis 1–11 biblical glasses so they see the world through the lens of God's Word. Then they will understand they are looking at a fallen world, not the world as God made it. Then they will understand it was our sin that caused all these problems. It's not God's fault the world is the way it is — it's our fault. God stepped into history as the babe in a manger to save us from what we did to ourselves and this world.

The origin of all the basic entities of life and the universe are in Genesis. The origin of death is in Genesis.

> *And the LORD God commanded the man, saying, "You may surely eat of every tree of the garden, but of the tree of the knowledge of good and evil you shall not eat, for in the day that you eat of it you shall surely die"* (Genesis 2:16–17).

The Bible calls death an enemy.

> *The last enemy to be destroyed is death* (1 Corinthians 15:26).

Death is going to be thrown into the lake of fire one day.

> *Then Death and Hades were thrown into the lake of fire. This is the second death, the lake of fire* (Revelation 20:14).

One day there will be a new heavens and a new earth, a restoration where there will be no more death, disease, or suffering.

> *Whom heaven must receive until the time for restoring all the things about which God spoke by the mouth of his holy prophets long ago* (Acts 3:21).

> *But according to his promise we are waiting for new heavens and a new earth in which righteousness dwells* (2 Peter 3:13).

> *He will wipe away every tear from their eyes, and death shall be no more, neither shall there be mourning, nor crying, nor pain anymore, for the former things have passed away* (Revelation 21:4).

So death is an intrusion. It wasn't a part of the original creation. How can a Christian then believe in evolution and millions of years that involve death, disease, violence, and bloodshed? What the Bible teaches about the origin of death does not fit with the belief that death over millions of years was a part of the processes of producing all the life forms. These two things contradict each other. The idea of millions of years in our modern times primarily came from atheists and deists of the 18th and 19th centuries who wanted to explain the fossil record without any recourse to the supernatural. They wanted to explain this record by natural processes. Thus, they

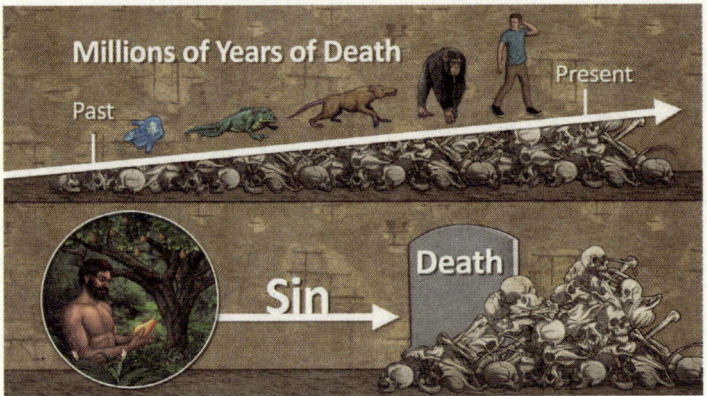

promoted the belief that the fossil-bearing layers were laid down slowly over millions of years, and this happened long before man. Many church leaders decided to accept these supposed millions of years and fit them into the Bible, developing ideas like the Gap Theory, Day-Age Theory, and many other compromise positions (e.g., Theistic Evolution [Evolutionary Creation], Progressive Creation, Framework Hypothesis, etc.).

Now, fossils are dead things, and the fossil record is replete with examples of diseases in the bones of various creatures. So when a Christian accepts evolution and/or millions of years, then they have accepted that there was death, bloodshed, and disease millions of years before man. They also are then saying that the death, bloodshed, and disease we see today has been going on for millions of years, and God called all that "very good."

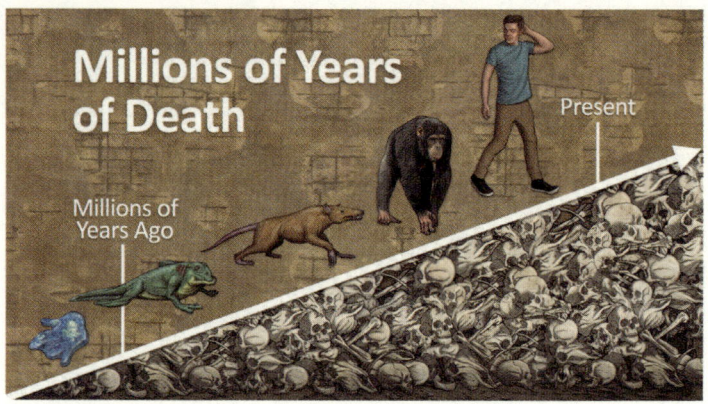

Millions of Years of Death

Millions of Years Ago

Present

But what did God do when Adam sinned? He made garments of skins and clothed Adam and Eve.

And the LORD God made for Adam and for his wife garments of skins and clothed them (Genesis 3:21).

God must have killed an animal(s) and shed its blood to clothe Adam and Eve. This is the origin of clothing. Why do we wear clothes? Animals don't wear clothes, but humans do because we're not animals. We are different, being made in God's image. God gave clothes because of sin, because sin distorts all of our thinking. Sin distorts everything. Now there has to be a covering. Also, that covering was symbolic of the fact that God would provide a way to take away our sin so we could live with our Creator forever.

This is the sacrifice scene at the Creation Museum for the second C (Corruption) of the 7 C's walkthrough. This was the first blood sacrifice as a covering for their sin. It is a picture of what was to come in Jesus Christ, the Lamb of God, who takes away the sin of the world. God was setting up the sacrificial system that pointed to the promise of the Messiah in Genesis 3:15.

> *I will put enmity between you and the woman, and between your offspring and her offspring; he shall bruise your head, and you shall bruise his heel* (Genesis 3:15).

The Israelites sacrificed animals over and over. We don't sacrifice animals today because this original sacrifice pointed to the One who would be the ultimate sacrifice, the Messiah, the Lord Jesus Christ.

> *For the death he died he died to sin, once for all, but the life he lives he lives to God* (Romans 6:10).

Now the Bible tells us that *without the shedding of blood there is no forgiveness of sins* (Hebrews 9:22). And in Leviticus 17:11 we read:

> *For the life of the flesh is in the blood, and I have given it for you on the altar to make atonement for your souls, for it is the blood that makes atonement by the life.*

In other words, because we sinned in Adam and death is a consequence, our bodies die. But we are made in the image of God. We live inside our bodies, so the person (our soul) is not going to die. We're going to live forever. We're not like the animals. We are made in God's image but, because of sin, would be separated from God forever. But God wants us to live forever with Him. For this to happen, there has to be the payment for sin. There has to be reparations, and we can't pay reparations. Only God can do this because we're sinners. We can't pay for our own sin. Because death is a consequence of sin, there has to be the giving of a life to pay the penalty for sin.

A man brought sin and death into the world. A man would have to pay the penalty for sin and death. It's impossible for the blood of bulls and goats to take away our sins because we're not connected to the animals.

> *For it is impossible for the blood of bulls and goats to take away sins* (Hebrews 10:4).

An animal can't pay the penalty for our sin. It would have to be a human being, a man. It has to be one of us because we're all descendants of Adam. But we're all sinners, so it can't be one of us, and yet it has to be.

What did God do? Oh, *The Wonder of It All*, as the song title proclaims. God provided the solution — He stepped into history in the person of His Son to be the Godman, the perfect Godman, a member of the human race, our relative, to die on a Cross, be raised from the dead, and now offers the free gift of salvation.

Jesus Christ
"The Last Adam"
1 Cor. 15:45

For as in Adam all die, so also in Christ shall all be made alive.
1 Corinthians 15:22 (ESV)

"The First Adam"
1 Cor. 15:45

As another song title states, *Jesus Paid It All*. He paid the penalty for us. He paid those reparations needed. What an example for us as we think about others who have wronged us.

Just ponder these Scriptures:

> *But God shows his love for us in that while we were still sinners, Christ died for us* (Romans 5:8).

> *He himself bore our sins in his body on the tree, that we might die to sin and live to righteousness. By his wounds you have been healed* (1 Peter 2:24).

> *For by grace you have been saved through faith. And this is not your own doing; it is the gift of God* (Ephesians 2:8).

> *But he was pierced for our transgressions; he was crushed for our iniquities; upon him was the chastisement that brought us peace, and with his wounds we are healed* (Isaiah 53:5).

I have a challenge for those Christians who believe in millions of years. God tells us that without the shedding of blood, there is no remission of sins. So how can Christians accept millions of years of bloodshed before sin? The first shedding of blood was when God killed an animal(s) to make the coverings for Adam and Eve.

Now I have never said that if someone believes in millions of years, they can't be a Christian. Salvation is conditioned upon faith in Christ, not what one believes about the age of the earth. From our research and other statistics, I would say that a majority of church leaders and academics believe in millions of years, or say they allow for it, or it doesn't matter. However, I do believe that those Christians who believe in millions of years have a major problem that needs to be addressed.

As I stated earlier, the idea of millions of years came out of the atheism and deism of the 1700s and 1800s. Such people wanted to explain everything by natural processes (without God). Naturalism (which is in reality atheism) has become the foundation for our modern secular education system.

The belief is most of the fossil layers were laid down over the supposed millions of years before man and not during the Flood of Noah's day. As I've stated earlier, many church leaders added the millions of years into the Bible. Following the popularizing of millions of years, Darwin proposed his ideas of biological evolution. Then many church leaders added this to the Bible and said God used evolution. Next the idea of the big bang was popularized, and many church leaders added that to the Bible and said God used the big bang. Thus, many compromise positions fitting evolutionary ideas and/or millions of years into the Bible arose.

Sadly, children, teens, and adults in many churches were told they could believe in evolution and millions of years as long as they trust Christ as Savior. But this opens the door for these generations to begin to doubt God's Word and Genesis and eventually leads to unbelief regarding the rest of Scripture. This has had a devastating effect on the church. Now for those Christians who do believe in millions of years, let me challenge you with the following.

In the fossil record, which according to secularists was laid down millions of years before man, there are numerous examples of animals eating each other, such as bite marks and bones found inside stomachs.

However, the Bible clearly teaches that the animals and Adam and Eve were vegetarian before man sinned.

> *And God said, "Behold, I have given you every plant yielding seed that is on the face of all the earth, and every tree with seed in its fruit. You shall have them for food. And to every beast of the earth and to every bird of the heavens and to everything that creeps on the earth, everything that has the breath of life, I have given every green plant for food." And it was so* (Genesis 1:29–30).

Humans were not told they could eat animals until after the Flood, where God states that just as He gave plants to eat originally, from now on (He changed our diet) humans could eat meat:

Every moving thing that lives shall be food for you. And as I gave you the green plants, I give you everything (Genesis 9:3).

For those who believe in millions of years, consider the fact that there are many documented examples of evidence of diseases like cancer, tumors, arthritis, abscesses, and infections in animal remains in the fossil record. How could God call this "very good"? This is attacking the character of God.

Photograph of the larger hadrosaur vertebra in lateral view. The space that contained the overgrowth opens to the caudal surface of the vertebra.[1]

Dr. Hila May holds a hadrosaur vertebra.[2] (Fox News[3])

No, there wasn't any death or disease in in the world before sin. Such things are a consequence of sin. This means layers of fossils all over the earth can't have been laid down millions of years before man. They must have been laid down after Adam sinned. How do we explain all these fossils all over the world after Adam sinned? Where would we start to have a worldview to begin to understand this? Genesis 1–11.

In Genesis 6–9 we read about the events associated with the global Flood of Noah's day. If there was a global Flood, you'd find billions of dead things buried in rock layers laid down by water all over the earth. And that's what we find. Most of the fossil record is the graveyard of the worldwide Flood that occurred about 4,300 years ago. It is not the graveyard of millions of years.

Dealing with Racism

This is dealt with in detail in the book I coauthored entitled *One Race One Blood* (see Appendix 2). However, I

PEOPLE GROUPS

will give you a big picture perspective and again reiterate that to have the right worldview to begin to deal with such issues, one must start with Genesis 1–11.

There was an event that occurred about a hundred years after the Flood at the Tower of Babel.

People had rebelled against God again, so God gave different languages. About 70 family groups, which

BIBLICAL VIEW

ADAM & EVE	1 Corinthians 15:45 Genesis 3:20
SONS & DAUGHTERS	Genesis 5:4
NOAH & SONS	Genesis 9:17–19
PEOPLE AT THE TOWER OF BABEL	Genesis 11:8–9 Acts 17:26

1

RACE

DIFFERENT PEOPLE GROUPS/CULTURES

means probably 70 language groups, moved away from each other, forming the different cultural groups and nations that we have today.

All humans are descendants of Noah back to Adam and Eve. This means biologically there is only one race of humans, Adam's race. So there are not different races of people, but different people groups that formed as a result of this event.

We are told that all human beings since the Flood are descendants of Noah's three sons. This links us all to Noah and back to Adam:

> *The sons of Noah who went forth from the ark were Shem, Ham, and Japheth. (Ham was the father of Canaan.) These three were the sons of Noah, and from these the people of the whole earth were dispersed* (Genesis 9:18–19).

As people groups moved away from each other, depending on who married whom, what combinations of DNA they received, and who died out, eventually specific external characteristics (that represent a small percentage of human genetic information) arose. Even skin shade (all humans are the same basic color from the main pigment melanin — a brown pigment) is a minor difference genetically.

What I so want Christians to understand is that we need to be raising up generations to know what they

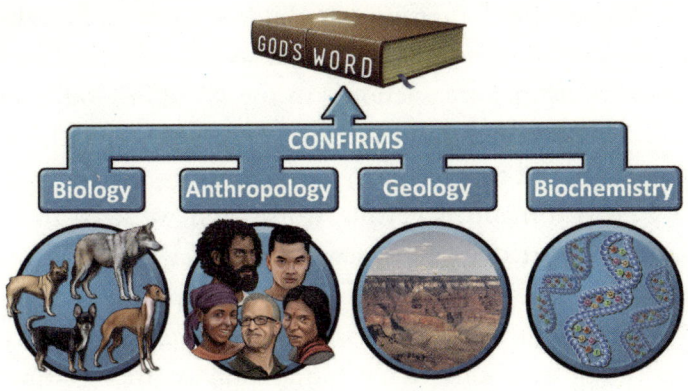

believe and why; understand how to think correctly with a Christian worldview; and have answers in biology, geology, anthropology, biochemistry, and so on to

counter the secular attacks of our day that are being used to undermine the authority of God's Word.

We need to be raising our children to think foundationally starting from God's Word so that when we have generations that are anchored to the Word of God, they will, we pray, withstand the tornado of moral relativism raging around us.

This tornado is getting worse, and we need to be more diligent than ever in watching over how we raise the coming generations and equip God's people today.

Be careful where your kids are educated and who is educating your kids. What foundation are they getting? Do you really know what's happening?

What Should We Do?

Pastors and parents: While we certainly should shield our children from some of the depravity and foolishness of the world, it's foolish to shield them from everything. Rather, we should use age-appropriate examples of what's going on in the culture right now to teach foundational thinking and help them build a truly biblical worldview. Don't bring it back to your opinions on the topic — bring it back to what the authority, God's Word, says.

ENDNOTES

1   Credit: Assaf Ehrenreich, Sackler

2   Credit: Tel Aviv University

3   Chris Claccia, "Cancer seen in humans also found in 66M-year-old dinosaur fossil," Fox News, February 17, 2020, https://www.foxnews.com/science/cancer-humans-found-dino-saur-fossil

Chapter Seven

THE SAND VERSUS THE ROCK

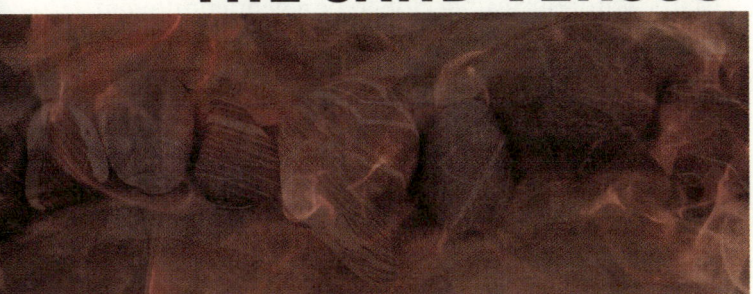

L et us summarize the battle.

Two foundations, two worldviews.

- Man's word: Darwin taught there were different races, some lower, some higher.
- God's Word: one race.

- Man's word: define marriage however you want.
- God's Word: marriage, one man and one woman.

- Man's word: one can decide to be a gender different than their biological sex and can use chemicals and bodily mutilation to accomplish that.
- God's Word: gender, two in humans.

- Man's word: get rid of spare cats, get rid of spare kids. We're just animals. Abortion is health care.
- God's Word: abortion, killing a human being made in the image of God.

Think about it. If we have generations in our churches, homes, and colleges that haven't been given the right foundation to develop a truly Christian worldview, when we try to give them the doctrines of Christianity, that structure won't stand.

They will end up building a different worldview from the wrong foundation they have from the world.

To sum it all up, I use castle diagrams.

On the right we have the rock of God's Word, which is foundational to the Christian castle. Now that rock

consists of Genesis 1–11 as the foundation for the rest of the Bible, our Christian worldview, and our doctrines and what we believe.

On the left we have the sand of man's word, the foundation for the secular worldview of moral relativism. The devil knows to use the Genesis 3 attack we have discussed. So what would be the method to attack the Christian castle? Attack the foundation of God's Word. And in this era, the attack is particularly leveled at Genesis 1–11. But sadly, many Christians who are on the Christian castle have compromised God's Word in Genesis 1–11 and are, in reality, attacking their own foundation. This is the most devastating attack of all. Compromise destroys! We see the castle crumbling.

But then Christians look at what they believe are the problems in the culture that we need to deal with —

gay "marriage," abortion, racism, etc. But they are not different problems, they are all symptoms of the same problem. The problem is the wrong foundation of man's word. Too many Christians have tried to deal with the symptoms instead of dealing with the wrong foundation and raising up generations on the right foundation of God's Word.

What we do at the ministry of Answers in Genesis and the Ark Encounter and Creation Museum is to help Christians raise up generations founded on the rock of God's Word, with Genesis 1–11 as the foundation so they can build a truly Christian worldview. We want to help God's people raise up generations who know what they believe and why. We equip them with answers to defend the Christian faith and knowledge on how to counter the wrong foundation and thus the resulting wrong (anti-God) worldview that is a consequence of a wrong foundation. We can't just deal with the symptoms (gay "marriage," abortion, racism, etc.); we must discover the foundational reason for why the symptoms exist. As a ministry and through our attractions, we are also challenging non-Christians with the truth of God's Word and the gospel.

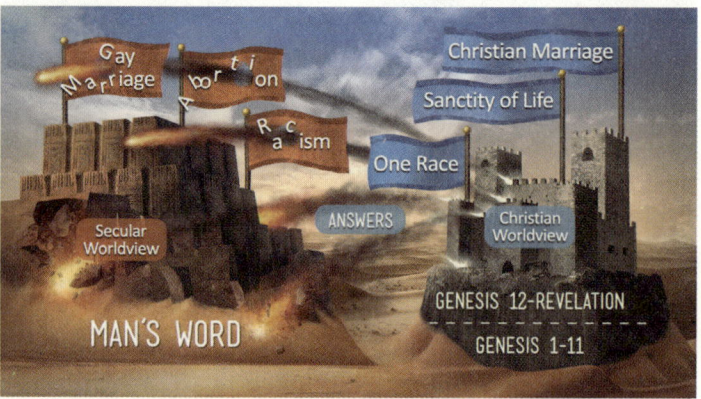

Let's think about this practically in regard to the nation we live in. Consider the abortion issue — a symptom of a wrong foundation. Changing laws to protect the sanctity of life is important, but it's not the ultimate solution. A perfect illustration of this is summed up in this headline in America: "Biden to roll back Trump's pro-life policies, introduce new pro-abortion legislation." Many Christians very rightly rejoiced at the pro-life actions under President Trump's administration. But the new administration as of 2021 places no value on the lives of unborn humans and is planning on rolling back those protections to allow more mothers to murder their unborn children as easily and freely as possible. In other words, ever-changing politics is not the ultimate answer!

The ultimate answer is the gospel of Jesus Christ and the truth of God's Word. You see, hearts and minds are changed when people have the right foundation of God's Word and come to recognize that they are sinners in need of a Savior and that Jesus paid the penalty for their sin with His death on the Cross. When we receive this free gift, we receive the Holy Spirit, who sanctifies us and opens up His Word to us so that we can understand its truth, which teaches the value of all human life — including the lives of unborn humans (see Psalm 139 for example). It's the gospel that heals broken lives, forgives us of all our sins, and gives us a new heart to love and serve others (including unborn children) as Christ has loved us.

Now, this is not to say Christians shouldn't lobby for just laws, seek to overturn unjust laws, and vote with unborn lives in mind — we can, and we should. But we shouldn't put our hope in that or replace sharing the gospel with political activism. Our hope and ultimate focus should be in the gospel of Jesus Christ and sharing that precious message with others (as so many Christians do, including those who run or volunteer at pregnancy care centers), even as we seek to overturn murderous laws.

The Right Way to Argue

In these days we live in, when Christians state that abortion is wrong and gay "marriage" is sin, invariably we will be accused of hate speech. When proclaiming a Christian morality, Christians will be accused of being misogynist, homophobic, and many other terms. I believe one of the reasons this happens is because many Christians have communicated their worldview in the wrong way.

Think about what we've been discussing. If a person has the foundation for man's word, then when a Christian proclaims the Christian worldview to them, they see it as Christians trying to impose their morality on them. They claim that is hate speech. Therein lies a big problem. Because the foundation through the culture has by and large changed to that of man's word, Christians can't try to change the way these people think from the top down. It won't work. It's a foundational problem. And because much of the church has allowed this foundational change, it's now resulted in that tornado of moral relativism permeating the culture. The change is happening at warp speed. Nonetheless, Christians need to understand the foundational problem and deal with the issues from the bottom up.

There are two practical examples to illustrate what I mean. The first was at a conference and a young man approached me to challenge me. The conversation went something like this:

> *"I'm gay, what are you going to say about that?"*
>
> I replied, *"Well, let me explain to you why I believe what I do. I start with the Bible as the foundation for my thinking."*
>
> The young man responded, *"Don't give me that Bible stuff; I don't believe the Bible."*
>
> I replied, *"Why don't you believe the Bible? Tell me why you think the Bible is wrong."*
>
> The young man said, *"We live in a scientific age, and science has disproved the Bible . . . it's just myth."*
>
> Now we are getting to the foundational problem. This is what we need to do — get the battle to where it's really at.
>
> I then asked, *"What specifically in science do you think proves the Bible is wrong?"*

The conversation continued for quite some time. He brought up all sorts of objections, which is why we need to have answers. Actually, I find (as I did with this young man) that most people who oppose the Bible (or even those Christians who oppose a literal Genesis) only regurgitate what they have heard or been taught. Most can't logically argue their position and back it up with real information they understand. Make sure you are equipped with answers to the most-asked questions of our day. This means be prepared for today's Genesis 3 attack. After I did my best to answer as many questions as I could, I then said something like:

> *"I've answered as many questions as I can for you. It seems you don't even want the answers with the way you are reacting. But, regardless, I do believe the Bible is the Word of God, a revelation from God to us to enable us to have the right foundation for our thinking. My worldview comes from this foundation."*

I then went on to say where what I believe about marriage comes from. I did the same with abortion and other issues as I've outlined in this book. Then I explained to him that if he didn't believe God's Word and believed man is just the result of natural processes, I understand why he would have a totally different worldview than me. He began to understand that our clash of worldviews was because we had two different starting points.

At one point he said something like, *"So you're admitting you start with the Bible."* I said that of course I do, that's where my worldview comes from. I then explained that until we both have the same starting point, we will never agree at the worldview level. Once he understood I believed his worldview was consistent with his foundation and I understood why he believed differently than me, he calmed down. I've found this approach usually takes the emotionalism out of the argument. We left it at the point where he said, *"Well, if the Bible is not true, then your worldview is false."* I agreed but told him the Bible is true. And then I also spoke to him about the message of the Bible and our sin and need for salvation. After all, the gospel is the most important message of all. He listened and thanked me for the conversation and left.

As you teach people foundationally, keep reminding them that if someone doesn't have the same foundation of God's Word, they will have a different worldview.

My second example is when I had the privilege of speaking at a secular university where the LGBTQ+ group had opposed me. I was invited by a Christian group to make a presentation. My invitation was subsequently withdrawn because of opposition, but through many different circumstances, the invitation was extended for the presentation to be a public one at the university. One of our scientists, Dr. Georgia Purdom, and I divided the presentation into two sections.

Throughout my presentation, I explained why I believed what I did about morality, the gospel, death, and so on. I hammered home that if someone didn't have the foundation of God's Word as I did, then I understood why that person would have a different foundation than me.

However, at the end of our presentations, questions were invited from the audience. One question came from a member of the LGBTQ+ group who said they were a Christian:

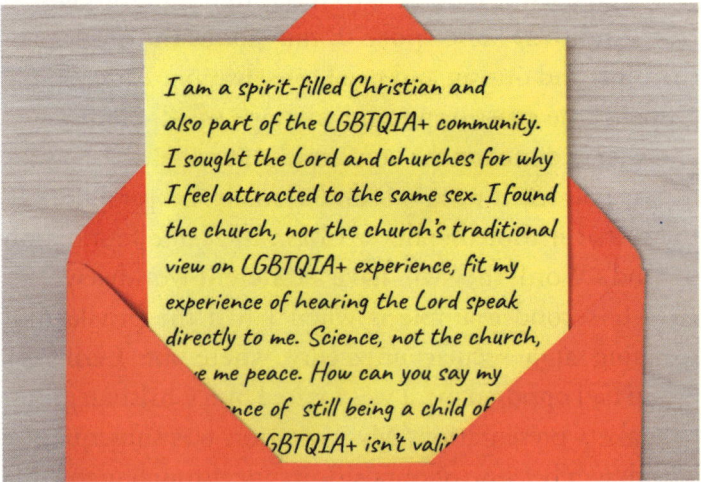

I am a spirit-filled Christian and also part of the LGBTQIA+ community. I sought the Lord and churches for why I feel attracted to the same sex. I found the church, nor the church's traditional view on LGBTQIA+ experience, fit my experience of hearing the Lord speak directly to me. Science, not the church, ‚e me peace. How can you say my ‚nce of still being a child of ‚GBTQIA+ isn't vali‚

This is the question: *"I am a spirit-filled Christian and also part of the LGBTQIA+ community. I sought the Lord and churches for why I feel attracted to the same sex. I found the church, nor the church's traditional view on LGBTQIA+ experience, fit my experience of hearing the Lord speak directly to me. Science, not the church, gave me peace. How can you say my experience of still being a child of God and LGBTQIA+ isn't valid?"*

I then answered something like this:

"During this presentation, I have been emphasizing God's written Word, the Bible. I have been showing that I start with God's Word and build my worldview. Now you say that God spoke to you. If this is the same God, then His spoken word can't be contradictory to His written Word. So you and I must have a different interpretation of God's Word beginning in Genesis. So we would need to sit down and deal with why we interpret God's Word differently. Until we sort that out and come to an agreement there, we will never solve our worldview clash. And I also want to add that just because I have a different worldview to someone does not mean I hate them. God's Word tells me clearly to 'love the Lord your God with all your heart and with all your soul and with all your strength and with all your mind, and your neighbor as yourself' [Luke 10:27]. We are all one family, one race going back to Adam. We need to treat each other as family."

It was interesting that the audience clapped when I said we should treat each other as family. And, of course, we should.

What Should We Do?

Pastors and parents: Teach your church congregations and your family how to argue from a foundational perspective so they can effectively share the gospel with others and love them as Christ does. Understanding the battle of foundations helps them understand why we think differently from the world and why those people aren't our enemies. They are lost people who desperately need Christ.

Chapter Eight

TAKE A BOLD STAND

We live in a time when I find many in the church know there is something dreadfully wrong with our culture and see a problem in their families and churches with the coming generations being more secular and leaving the church. But so many don't understand what the problem is and how to deal with it. I pray this book will open people's eyes as to what has happened, why it has happened, and how to go about dealing with it as we should.

I also have found many Christian leaders are not willing to take a bold stand in their churches for God's Word beginning in Genesis. Many times over the years I've had pastors come to me and say that a couple of the well-known people in their church were offended by what I had said in my talk, and could I be less authoritative in how I say things. They intimated that I could tell them if they believe differently that's okay, as we can agree to differ. One pastor said I needed to say if people believed in millions of years, then that's okay, as there are different interpretations. So, because a couple of people in the church compromised God's Word, I had to change my talk to allow their view to be a valid one. No, I will not do that. I don't accuse those people of not being Christian. But I will speak authoritatively from Scripture. I've been amazed (and distressed) at the number of times such things have happened. Pastors need to have the courage to speak what is right from Scripture even if some people (and their checkbooks) leave the church. Most Christians in our churches want authoritative teaching. They want to know what to believe and why and be equipped. I'm often reminded of what we read about Jesus and the people He spoke to as the Godman:

> *And when Jesus finished these sayings, the crowds were astonished at his teaching, for he was teaching them as one who had authority, and not as their scribes* (Matthew 7:28–29).

May we have the boldness of Paul as he taught the Scriptures,

> *proclaiming the kingdom of God and teaching about the Lord Jesus Christ with all boldness and without hindrance* (Acts 28:31).

And may we never be like the Pharisees Jesus referred to in John 12:43,

> *for they loved the praise of men more than the praise of God* (NKJV).

Epilogue by Denise Kissee

I am honored to recommend this book by one of God's most gifted teachers of the holy Scriptures. Ken Ham's teaching is so practical and understandable and on a level that both adults and children can relate to.

I direct the Vacation Bible School program at my church, First Baptist Church Woodstock. Several years ago, we switched to using Answers VBS, Answers in Genesis' VBS curriculum, and it's made such a powerful difference. Here's what comes to mind when I think of it: apologetics, meaty teaching, biblical authority, real life application, and fun.

So many children's materials teach Scripture as just a collection of stories or moral tales. This leaves children with both a shallow understanding of Scripture and of the authority the Word of God holds over our lives. It's hard to find materials for children that are biblically sound, authoritative, and, of course, fun!

Answers VBS incorporates all of that and more with their approach. And it really resonates with the children. They love hearing answers to the questions of our day. They love getting meaty answers that add substance to their faith. It helps give them a confidence in trusting God's Word. They love doing the science experiments (a wonderful, unique element of Answers VBS), showing that Christians love science. They love singing the theologically rich, catchy songs and learning the Scripture memory verses. After a week in VBS, children have gleaned such depth from God's Word, not merely had a week of fun (though they certainly have that too!). We've seen kids grow in the knowledge of the Lord and even come to faith in Christ during VBS week. Even parents are impacted.

One of my favorite teachings during my time directing VBS has been the focus on "one God, one Savior, and one Lord." Even though we used the curriculum that taught that years ago, it has stuck with me! I feel this is one of the greatest doctrinal principles that needs to be taught, as in today's culture, to say "I believe in God" could mean many different things. It's teachings like these, that directly address the issues of our day, that make Answers VBS so powerful to the children (and those who teach it!).

I'm not writing this as just as an endorsement of Answers VBS, but rather to emphasize to churches how important it is to use the approach to teaching God's Word that Mr. Ham has laid out in this book and is used in their many resources such as the VBS program. Mr. Ham has done a phenomenal job in drawing the parallel and importance of teaching the kids the Bible and teaching the kids that the Bible is history.

We can't continue to just teach the Bible the way so many churches and families have for past generations. We live in a different, very secularized culture. The Bible is not merely a collection of stories or moral tales. It's the infallible, authoritative word of our Creator. And kids need to know that and know that they can trust what it says and be ready for the attacks the world levels at the Scriptures.

I have shared these principles with leaders around the country, telling them that children are going to school to learn "history" and to church to learn "stories." We have to do a better job at tying the two together, helping children understand that the Bible is history and that it applies to the world around us and our day-to-day life.

Our culture has set itself up as the authority, telling us what is "right" and "wrong." But what they say is "right and wrong" is constantly changing, based on the whims of those in rebellion against God. Our children are caught in this ever-changing climate of cultural opinion. Sadly, many buy into the thinking of our day and drift from the faith their churches and parents worked to instill in them. God's Word is attacked in so many ways, and our kids need to be trained to stand firm on God's Word.

We've seen how teaching God's Word authoritatively (which is how Scripture presents itself) and foundationally, using apologetics (answers to the attacks of our day), and helping children understand that God's Word is the foundation for a Christian worldview helps ground them in their faith. It helps them see through the lies of our culture and remain committed to what the Word of God clearly teaches.

This foundational approach is what is needed in our churches and in teaching our children. I am confident when I use Answers in Genesis' curriculum that I'm giving my children biblical principles that are doctrinally sound. As our previous pastor, Dr. Johnny Hunt, once said about the Answers VBS program, "What a difference it makes to make much of God's Word." Indeed, what a difference it does make! A difference with an eternal impact.

Denise Kissee

Director of Elementary Ministries

First Baptist Woodstock, GA

Epilogue by Dr. Joseph Boot

Over the years, as I have made Genesis and God's law-Word for creation central to my teaching and apologetic, God has poured out His blessing. By God's grace, fruitfulness and effectiveness in sharing and defending the faith evangelistically as well as teaching the biblical world-and-life-view to deepen people's understanding has been the result. Ken Ham has blazed a trail in this regard. The ministry of Answers in Genesis has consistently been a source of blessing and encouragement to God's people in equipping them to evangelize as well as teach a scriptural world-and-life-view that stands upon the Word of God from the very first verse.

For as long as I can remember, right back to my high school years, I have always had an interest in the question of origins and the basic challenge of the evolutionary paradigm to the Christian faith — it was something I vigorously debated with unbelieving friends even in school as a young Christian. That interest led me to seek out resources that were faithfully addressing the issue, which in those days were relatively few compared to what is available now, thanks to ministries like AiG. Pursuing that interest, I remember the first time I heard Ken Ham speak — which was over 25 years ago now at a church in Scotland — and then a few years later reading his interesting primer, *Creation Evangelism*.

What I particularly appreciated all those years back was Ken's focus on the "big picture," the "grand narrative," of Scripture and the simple fact that the message of *redemption* only made sense in the broader context of special creation and the subsequent fall of man into sin, death, and ruin. This teaching really rang true in my mind and gripped my heart in the early years.

I will always be thankful that Ken and AiG helped me to realize that creation and redemption stand in an historical continuum; they are involved in each other and cannot be artificially separated into sealed-off domains. This means that what we believe about creation is determinative for what we believe about the nature, scope, and character of redemption itself. The profound scriptural foundation of the Christian faith, discerned in the creation, fall, redemption, and consummation of all things through Christ, has stayed with me throughout my ministry. In my formative years, Ken Ham's faithful work in addressing the relevance and power of the Bible's teaching on creation helped reinforce to me the vital importance of a robust *biblical worldview*. It finally led me to an appreciation of the truth of Abraham Kuyper's most well-known statement, "There is not a square inch in the whole domain of our human existence over which Christ, who is Sovereign over all, does not cry, 'This is Mine!' " Christ is our Lord and redeemer because He is first our Creator and Sustainer who is bringing all things to their appointed conclusion by the reconciliation of all things to God — a work that will be complete when the last enemy, death, is defeated (1 Cor. 15:24–28).

As a cultural apologist and pastor who has found myself at home within the reformational tradition and soundly in favor of a transcendental approach to defending the Christian philosophy of life (immanent and transcendental criticism), I have sometimes been represented by other Christians as having a minimal interest in the external evidences of the Christian worldview — evidence like the authenticity of biblical manuscripts, the ways that Christ fulfilled Old Testament prophecies, or, significantly for this epilogue, the many compelling arguments for special creation as taught in the narrative history of Genesis. While it is true that my own cultural apologetics ministry has not emphasized the fascinating evidence of biblical creation but has focused on a philosophical and cultural critique of unbelieving worldviews (including the evolutionary worldview), it would be a mistake to assume from that fact that I consider them unimportant.

The reason I have adopted and taught a transcendental — what is sometimes called a presuppositional, or worldview — approach to apologetics is partly because of my conviction that all of life in all of its aspects is undergirded with pre-theoretical religious commitments. In other words, none of us approach the data of our experience from a truly neutral point of view; we all have assumptions about the world that colour our perspective and shape our conclusions. The data or facts to be regarded as "evidence" are already being interpreted in terms of a particular view of reality. This means that for evidence to be most powerful and convincing, it should be openly set in the context of a broader world-and-life-view. This is the primary area in which I have sought to make a contribution to the defense of the faith. Another reason for my chosen focus is simply that I do not have a background in the natural sciences beyond high school, and so do not possess the necessary training to speak in depth on the matters of the natural sciences in a technical way. My interest has focused more upon the philosophy of science.

Yet it is this very thing that I have most appreciated about Ken Ham over the years — he balances offering scientific evidence with a keen awareness of the deeper questions of world-and-life-view that are at play with the issue of origins and in the contemporary West in general. In a way, Ken and I have been approaching the same root issue along slightly different tracks but from the same starting point: a steadfast commitment to the full authority and trustworthiness of the Word of God in its totality. As Ken has demonstrated well in these pages, to compromise that Word with pagan ideas in the name of helping people believe the gospel or become accepting of Scripture turns out to be abortive. All attempts at a *synthesis* of particles-to-people evolution and special creation are not only intellectually dissatisfying, they fail to win the acceptance of an unbelieving world, and they only sow confusion and unbelief in an area where clarity is the thing desperately called for. This should not surprise us, for as we have seen since our first parents rebelled in the Garden of God, when we twist or adulterate God's Word, everyone loses.

For decades, Ken has faithfully and persistently challenged the prevailing evolutionary worldview from a position of bold, straightforward confidence in the Word of God and has equipped thousands of Christians to do the same. As he has shown in this book, our attitude toward the evolutionary view of reality is not abstract but has serious and far-reaching implications for all of life. When I noticed in the early pages the key point that it only takes one generation to lose a culture, I knew right away that Ken has clearly seen that there is a deep spiritual crisis going on at the civilizational level in the West, profoundly affecting the foundational assumptions of our society. At the root of that crisis is a denial of *creational normativity* — that God has created all things after their kind and governs all things in terms of His law-Word. If we would hope to correct this suicidal course in our apostate era, we must get *creation* right.

As founding pastor at Westminster Chapel and founder and president of the Ezra Institute, we have often described this cultural problem as an increasingly *systematic unbelief*. The present cultural situation expresses a pre-theoretical commitment to other gods. We are living in open denial of the living God who transcends cosmic time (creation) and whose binding Word-revelation is manifest in creation, incarnate in Christ and laid down in the Scriptures. This apostate secular faith does not confine itself to a narrow, intellectual realm, as though the question of the origin of all things were of purely academic interest. Rather, by turning to a pagan evolutionary worldview, a world of flux that denies the personal creating, governing, and sustaining Word of Christ, our culture is making foundational and dogmatic claims about what it means to be human. In turn, a culture's answer to that question informs the way it will approach every fundamental issue from identity, marriage, and sexuality to law, justice, education, the role of the state, abortion, euthanasia, and much more. Indeed, it is hard to imagine any matter that is not ultimately related back to our answer to the question of origin — and not simply the why of our origin but the how.

Against this present state of affairs in the West, I have often emphasized the need for a countervailing *systematic belief*. We cannot fight something with nothing. A mish-mash of autobiographical spiritual experiences and devotional anecdotes combined with knowledge of some Bible stories does not constitute a coherent scriptural view of reality. There is a distinctly Christian way to think about every area of life, and that must begin with a commitment to the trustworthiness and authority of God's revelation, beginning with Genesis and the entirety of the biblical teaching about creation. On this basis, we can develop a coherent and consistent worldview and witness that strikes at the root of unbelief and enables people to see the reality, truth, and beauty of the gospel of the kingdom. This is something that Ken clearly understands. The inescapable result of rejecting the starting point of Scripture is to leave the believer without a firm foundation for believing or defending anything.

The apostle Paul wrote to his young disciple Timothy, *"All Scripture is given by inspiration of God, and is profitable for doctrine, for reproof, for correction, for instruction in righteousness, that the man of God may be complete, thoroughly equipped for every good work"* (2 Tim. 3:16–17; NKJV).

Dr. Joseph Boot
Founding pastor at Westminster
Chapel in Toronto
Founder and President of The Ezra
Institute for Contemporary
Christianity

Statement of Faith

The Answers in Genesis Statement of Faith is included so it can be used as a guide for Christian leaders/organizations in constructing a robust statement for the times we live in.

In order to preserve the function and integrity of the Answers in Genesis (AiG) ministry (and its various attractions and outreaches, both domestic and international) in its mission to proclaim the absolute truth and authority of Scripture and to provide a biblical role model to our employees and to the global body of Christ, the community, and society at large, it is imperative that all persons employed by the AiG ministry in any capacity, or who serve as volunteers, should abide by and agree to our Statement of Faith and conduct themselves accordingly.

The Triune God

- There is one God, self-existent and eternal, infinitely perfect, the Creator, Sustainer, and Ruler of all things (Genesis 1:1, 1:23, 2:1–4; Deuteronomy 6:4, 33:27; Psalm 22:28, 103:19, 147:5; Isaiah 40:28, 45:18; Daniel 5:21; 2 Samuel 22:31; Nehemiah 9:6; Ecclesiastes 12:1–6; Matthew 5:48, 28:18; Mark 12:29–34; John 1:1–3; 1 Corinthians 8:4; Romans 16:26; Colossians 1:16–17, 2:3; Hebrews 1:1–3, 9:14; 2 Peter 4:9; Revelation 1:8, 4:11).

- The Godhead is triune: one God, three Persons: God the Father, God the Son, and God the Holy Spirit. Each Person is fully God, their glory equal and their majesty coeternal (Genesis 1:1–2; Matthew 3:15–17; John 1:1–3).

- For his own glory and by his own decree, the triune God created heaven and earth, time, and all things, visible and invisible, living and nonliving, material and nonmaterial (Genesis 1:1–2:3; Exodus 20:11, 31:17; Isaiah 46:9–10; Nehemiah 9:6; 1 Timothy 1:17; Colossians 1:16; Revelation 22:13).

- Our Lord Jesus Christ, the uncreated Creator and only begotten Son of God, took on human flesh to be fully man without ever ceasing to be fully God (Luke 24:39; John 1:1–3, 1:14, 1:18, 3:16, 8:58; Colossians 1:16; Acts 2:22; 1 Corinthians 15:47; Philippians 2:5–8; Hebrews 1:1–3).

- Jesus Christ was conceived by the Holy Spirit, born of the virgin Mary, and lived a sinless life (Isaiah 7:14, 53:4–6; Matthew 1:16–23; John 8:29, 8:46; 2 Corinthians 5:21; 1 Peter 2:21–22).

- Jesus died on the cross, making a full and satisfactory atonement for man's sin. (Matthew 1:16–23; Luke 1:30–31; John 19:30; 1 Thessalonians 1:10; Hebrews 9:11–12, 10:12–14; 1 Peter 1:17–18; 1 John 2:2).

- Jesus Christ rose bodily from the dead, ascended to heaven, is currently seated at the right hand of God the Father as our Intercessor, and shall return in person (bodily and visibly) to this earth as Judge of the living and the dead (1 Corinthians 15:3–5; Acts 17:31; Ephesians 1:17–23; 2 Timothy 4:1; Hebrews 7:25).

- The scientific aspects of creation are important but are secondary in importance to the proclamation of the gospel of Jesus Christ as Sovereign, Creator, Redeemer, and Judge (1 Corinthians 15:3–5).

- The Holy Spirit, the third Person of the Godhead, is Lord and Giver of life, who glorifies our Lord Jesus Christ and convicts the world of sin, righteousness, and judgment (John 15:26, 16:8–11, 16:14).

- The Holy Spirit's work is necessary for sinners to repent and believe in Jesus Christ through the gospel call (Romans 8; 1 Corinthians 2:6–14, 12:3; Titus 3:3–7).

- The Holy Spirit lives and works in each believer to produce the fruits of righteousness (John 14:16–17; Acts 1:8, 4:31; Romans 8:11; 1 Corinthians 3:16, 6:18–20; Galatians 5:22–23; Ephesians 2:19–22).

- The Triune God has revealed himself in Scripture in the male gender with masculine pronouns and masculine titles such as Father, Son, God, King, Priest, and Prophet (Psalm 5:2; Matthew 28:19; John 14:26).

Scripture

- The 66 books of the Bible are the unique, written Word of God. The Bible is divinely inspired, inerrant, infallible, supremely authoritative, and sufficient in everything it teaches. Its assertions are factually true in all the original autographs. Its authority is not limited to spiritual, religious, or redemptive themes but includes its assertions in such fields as history and science (Deuteronomy 4:2, 12:32; 2 Timothy 3:16–17; Revelation 22:18–19).

- The final guide to the interpretation of Scripture is Scripture itself (Proverbs 8:8–9; Matthew 12:3–5, 19:4, 22:31; Mark 7:13, 12:10, 12:26; Luke 6:3; 2 Corinthians 4:2; 2 Timothy 3:16–17).

- All things necessary for our salvation are expressly and clearly taught in Scripture (foundation of the gospel: Genesis 1:1, 1:31, 3:17–19; Romans 5:12, 3:23; presenting the gospel: 1 Corinthians 15:1-4; Romans 6:23, 10:9; John 3:14–18; Acts 16:30–31; Ephesians 2:8; Romans 5:1–2).

Origins and History

- The account of origins presented in Genesis 1–11 is a simple but factual presentation of actual events, and therefore, provides a reliable framework for scientific research into the question of the origin and history of life, mankind, the earth, and the universe.

- The various original life forms (kinds), including mankind, were made by direct, supernatural, creative acts of God (i.e., not by natural, physical processes over millions of years). The living descendants of any of the original kinds (apart from man) may represent more than one species today, reflecting the genetic potential within each original kind. Only limited biological changes (including mutational deterioration) have occurred naturally within each kind since creation (i.e., one kind does not change over time into a different kind: Genesis 1:11–12, 1:21, 1:24–25, 30:37–42; 1 Corinthians 15:39).

- The great flood of Genesis was an actual historic event, worldwide (global) in its extent and catastrophic in its effects. At one stage during the flood, the waters covered the entire surface of the whole globe with no land surface being exposed anywhere—the flood of Noah is not to be understood as any form of local or regional flood. The Noachian flood was a significant geological event, and most fossiliferous sediments were deposited at that time (Genesis 7:19–20; 2 Peter 3:5–7).

- Scripture teaches a recent origin of man and the whole creation, with history spanning approximately 4,000 years from creation to Christ.

- The days in Genesis do not correspond to geologic ages but are six consecutive, 24-hour days of creation; the first day began in Genesis 1:1, and the seventh day, which was also a normal 24-hour day, ended in Genesis 2:3 (Genesis 1:1–2:3; Exodus 20:8–11, 31:17; Hebrews 4:3–4).

- The gap theory, progressive creation, day-age, framework hypothesis, theistic evolution (i.e., evolutionary creation), functionality–cosmic temple, analogical days, day-gap-day, and any other views that try to fit evolution or millions of years into Genesis are incompatible with Scripture.

- The view, commonly used to evade the implications or the authority of biblical teaching, namely that knowledge and/or truth may be divided into secular and religious, is unbiblical and therefore should be rejected (1 Corinthians 10:31; Colossians 3:17; for more information, see https://answersingenesis.org/store/product/world-religions-and-cults-vol-3/).

- No apparent, perceived, or claimed evidence in any field of study, including science, history, and chronology, can be valid if it contradicts the clear teaching of Scripture obtained by historical-grammatical interpretation. Of primary importance is the fact that evidence is always subject to interpretation by fallible people who do not possess all information (Numbers 23:19; 2 Samuel 22:31; Psalm 18:30; Isaiah 46:9–10, 55:9; Romans 3:4; 2 Timothy 3:16).

Man

- Mankind, consisting of two genders (male and female), is created in the image of God. Each of these two distinct, complementary genders reflects the image of God (Genesis 1:26–27, 5:2, 9:6; Matthew 19:4–6; Mark 10:6; 1 Corinthians 11:7; James 3:9–10).

- The special and unique creation of Adam from dust and Eve from Adam's rib was supernatural and immediate. Adam and Eve did not originate from any other preexisting lifeforms (Genesis 2:7, 2:21–23, 3:19; 1 Corinthians 11:8–12, 15:47–49).

- All human life is sacred and begins at conception (defined as the moment of fertilization). Each unborn child is a unique, living human being, created in the image of God, and must be respected and protected both before and after birth. The abortion of an unborn child or the active, intentional taking of human life through euthanasia or assisted suicide constitutes a violation of the sanctity of human life and is a crime against God and man (Genesis 9:6; Exodus 20:13; Deuteronomy 5:17; Psalm 51:5; 1 Corinthians 15:49; James 2:11).

- There is only one race of mankind—the human race or Adam's race. Adam and Eve were the first two humans. All people alive today are the descendants of Adam and Eve and subsequently Noah (Genesis 1:26–27, 3:20, 10:1, 10:32; 1 Corinthians 14:45–47; Luke 17:27; Hebrews 11:7; 1 Peter 3:20; 2 Peter 2:5).

- Since all humans are made in the image of God, all humans have equal dignity and value regardless of age (including the unborn), intelligence, gender, physical ability, shade of skin tone, religion, ethnicity, or any other characteristic (Genesis 1:26–27, 3:20, 11:9; Acts 17:26–28).

- The concepts of "social justice," "intersectionality," and "critical race theory" are anti-biblical and destructive to human flourishing (Ezekiel 18:1–20; James 2:8–9).

- Parents are responsible to instruct their children in Christian faith and conduct, to set before them godly and consistent examples of the same, and in every way to "bring them up in the nurture and admonition of the Lord" (Deuteronomy 6:6–9; Proverbs 22:6; Ephesians 6:4).

- The only legitimate marriage, based on the creation ordinance in Genesis 1 and 2, sanctioned by God is the joining of one naturally born man and one naturally born woman in a single, exclusive union as delineated in Scripture. God intends sexual intimacy to only occur between a man and a woman who are married to each other and has commanded that no intimate sexual activity be engaged in outside of a marriage between a man and a woman. Any form of sexual immorality, such as adultery, fornication, prostitution, homosexuality, lesbianism, bisexual conduct, bestiality, incest, pornography, abuse, or any attempt to change one's gender, or disagreement with one's biological gender, is sinful and offensive to God (Genesis 1:27–28, 2:24; Matthew 5:27–30, 19:4-5; Mark 10:2–9; 1 Corinthians 6:9–11; Thessalonians 4:3–7; Hebrews 13:4).

- Gender and biological sex are equivalent and cannot be separated. A person's gender is determined at conception (fertilization), coded in the DNA, and cannot be changed by drugs, hormones, or surgery. Rejection of one's biological sex (gender) or identifying oneself by the opposite sex is a sinful rejection of the way God made that person. These truths must be communicated with compassion, love, kindness, and respect, pointing everyone to the truth that God offers redemption and restoration to all who confess and forsake their sin, seeking his mercy and forgiveness through Jesus Christ (Genesis 1:26–28, 5:1–2; Psalm 51:5, 139:13–16; Jeremiah 1:5; Matthew 1:20–21, 19:4–6; Mark 10:6; Luke 1:31; Acts 3:19–21; Romans 10:9–10; 1 Corinthians 6:9–11; Galatians 3:28).

Sin

- The special creation of Adam (the first man) and Eve (the first woman) and their subsequent fall into sin is the basis for the necessity of salvation for mankind (Genesis 2:7, 2:17, 2:22–23, 3:6–20; Romans 5:12; 1 Corinthians 15:45–49).

- Human death (both physical and spiritual) as well as all animal death, disease, bloodshed, suffering, extinction, thorns and thistles, and all other natural evils (e.g., earthquakes, hurricanes, tsunamis, etc.) entered this world subsequent to, and as a direct consequence of, man's sin (Genesis 2:16–17, 3:8, 3:19, 4:4–8; Romans 5:12, 8:20–22; 1 Corinthians 15:21–22).

- All mankind are sinners, inherently from Adam and individually (by choice), and are therefore subject to God's wrath and condemnation (1 Kings 8:46; Isaiah 53:6; Psalm 116:11; Proverbs 16:5; John 3:16–18, 12:48; Romans 3:23).

- Since all of mankind is made in God's image and also fallen, all humans are equally sinful, equally deserving of eternal punishment, and equally able to receive salvation in Christ (Isaiah 53:6; John 12:32; Romans 3:23, 5:12; 2 Peter 3:9).

Salvation

- The doctrines of Creator and Creation cannot ultimately be divorced from the gospel of Jesus Christ (John 1:1–3, 1:14–18; Colossians 1:13–20).

- Freedom from the penalty and power of sin is available to man only through the sacrificial death and shed blood of Jesus Christ and his complete and bodily resurrection from the dead (Luke 24:39; John 8:12, 8:36, 14:6; Acts 4:12; 1 Timothy 2:3–6; 1 Peter 1:3).

- Salvation is by God's grace alone, a gift received by faith alone in Christ alone (Ephesians 2:8–9; Titus 3:3–7).

- The one who is born of God has repented, recognized the death of Christ as full payment for sin, and received the risen Christ as Savior, Lord, and God (John 1:12–13; Acts 3:19, 16:31, 17:30–31, 20:21; Galatians 2:20–21; 1 John 3:9).

Church

- The church of Jesus Christ is composed of all who are united with him in saving faith and who are thus members of the body of which he is the head (John 3:16, 3:36, 11:25; Acts 16:30–31; Romans 10:8–10; Ephesians 5:23; Colossians 1:18).

- Those who do not believe in Christ are subject to everlasting, conscious punishment in hell, but believers are secure to enjoy eternal life with God in heaven (Matthew 15:49–50, 25:46; John 3:16–18, 3:36, 5:24; 1 Thessalonians 1:8–10; 1 John 5:11–13; Revelation 21:8).

- All Christians are to live in fellowship with a local, Bible-believing church (as portrayed in the New Testament), uniting in its worship of the triune God, supporting the great commission, and loving one another with pure and sincere hearts (Acts 20:7; 1 Corinthians 11:17–33, 16:2; Hebrews 10:23–25, 13:17).

Christ's Return

- Our Lord Jesus Christ will personally and bodily return in glory as he has promised, and he will consummate his kingdom. Christ will judge the living and the dead at his appearing (John 6:39–40, 12:48; Acts 1:9–11; 1 Peter 4:5).

- All shall be raised from the dead: those who have died in Christ to eternal life in heaven and those who have rejected him to conscious and everlasting punishment in the lake of fire (hell) (Daniel 12:2; Matthew 15:49–50, 25:41–46; Luke 12:5; 1 Corinthians 15:12–26; Revelation 21:8).

- Satan, who is a personal spiritual adversary of both God and mankind, will be judged and cast into the lake of fire (hell) for eternity (Matthew 25:41; Revelation 20:10).

(Updated: March 5, 2021)

Recommended apologetics resources:

The New Answers Books 1, 2, 3, and 4 and Flood of Evidence

These four *Answers* books, as well as the *Flood of Evidence*, are the five best-selling creation apologetics resources in the world. Together, these books contain detailed answers to 170 of the most-asked questions from people in today's world. These questions really cover the main objections that constitute the Genesis 3 attack of the 21st century.

Questions include:

Doesn't Carbon-14 Disprove the Bible? Could God Have Really Created Everything in Six Days? What Really Happened to the Dinosaurs? What's the Best "Proof" of Creation? How Should a Christian Respond to "Gay Marriage"? What about Satan and the Origin of Evil? Is Man the Cause of

Global Warming? Did Life Come from Outer Space? Why Did God Make Viruses? Dragons . . . Were They Real? Should We Be Concerned about Climate Change? What about Distant Starlight Models? Global or Local Flood? How Long Did It Take for Noah to Build the Ark? How Could Noah Get and Care for All the Animals? Where Did the Water for the Flood Come from and Where Did It Go? and many more.

How Do We Know the Bible Is True? Vol. 1 and 2

These two books contain answers to 59 of the most-asked questions people have relating to general Bible apologetics. *Questions include:*

How Do We Know the Bible Is True? Is the Trinity Three Different Gods? How Should We Interpret the Bible? What about the Factual Claims in The Da Vinci Code? How Did We Get the Bible in English? Polygamy in the Light of Scripture; Who Created God? Where Did God Come From? The "Missing" Old Testament Books; Has

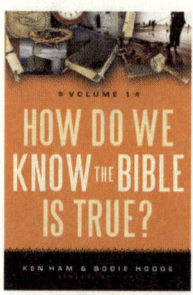 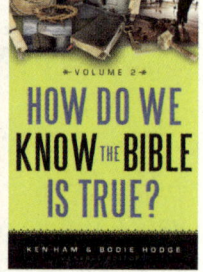

the Bible's Text Been Changed Over the Years? and many more.

Demolishing Supposed Bible Contradictions Vol. 1 and 2

These two books detail information to answer over 80 common objections to various passages in the Bible in regard to supposed contradictions, mistakes, etc.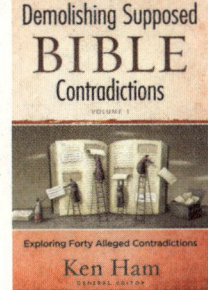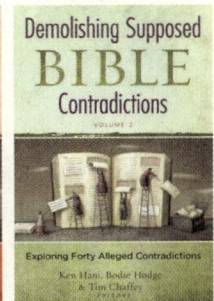
Topics include:
Can God be tempted?
Why don't Christians follow all the Old Testament laws? Is the earth immovably set on pillars or hanging on nothing? Does the Bible make a mistake in claiming that pi equals 3? Was Solomon really going to cut a baby in half? Does Genesis 1 teach the sky was solid? and many more.

World Religions and Cults Vol. 1, 2, and 3

Why do certain religions believe and practice what they do? How do they view the Bible? How do we deal with these religions from a biblical authority perspective? These three volumes deal with over 50 different religions and cults, giving detailed answers to equip Christians to be able to effectively witness to people caught up in such groups.
Groups covered include:
Islam, Jehovah's Witnesses, Judaism, Mormonism, Satanism, Freemasonry, New Age Movement, Hinduism,

Shinto, Buddhism, Atheism, Secular Humanism, Materialism, and many more.

Glass House

This book gives answers to the classic arguments for evolution and millions of years taught in public schools and colleges and universities.

Detailed answers are given to 27 questions including:

What Is Evolution? The Three Types to Recognize

Millions of Years: Where Did the Idea Come From?

Living Fossils

What about Natural Selection?

What about the Missing Links?

What about Human Evolution?

What about Bird Evolution — Aren't They Dinosaurs?

and many more.

One Race One Blood

This book reveals the origins of the horrors of discrimination, the biblical truth of "interracial" marriage, as well as the proof revealed in the Bible that God created only one race. Explore the science of genetics, melanin, and skin tone, affected by the history of the Tower of Babel and the origin of the people groups around the world. This

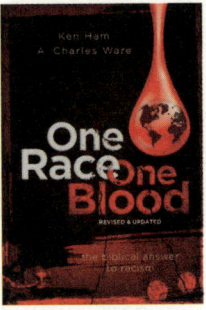

resource teaches "grace relations," not race relations.

The Lie

The Bible is the textbook of the Answers in Genesis ministry. *The Lie* is the classic textbook of the message of the ministry covering the relevance of Genesis.

Topics include:

> Genesis is the foundation for all biblical doctrine
> Can Christians believe in
>> evolution/millions of years
>> and add that to Genesis?
> What are the theological problems
>> for Christians who believe in
>> millions of years?
> Why does it matter what one
>> believes about Genesis?

What connection has Genesis to moral issues like
gender, abortion, gay "marriage," etc.?

Genesis 1–11 is literal history and the foundation for
the rest of the Bible, all doctrine, and a Christian
worldview.

Gospel Reset

How can we evangelize a very secularized culture? This book details
the difference between how the
gospel was presented to the Jews in
Acts 2 and the Greeks in Acts 17. A
comparison is made with the West
for the older generations being
more like an Acts 2 culture and the
younger generations being more like an Acts 17 culture.
To evangelize an Acts 17–type culture means changing
the way the gospel has been presented in the past. The
culture has changed. Christian values, traditions, and
terminologies that were once common knowledge have
become a thing of the past. This book will help you effectively share the message of salvation to a more "Greek-
ized" culture.

Will They Stand — Parenting Kids to Face the Giants

How should we educate our children? How should we
be training them? What are the roles for fathers and

mothers in bringing up children? Should kids from church homes be sent to public schools to be witnesses for the Lord? What does God's Word say about the priorities and methods parents should use in the education of children? How do parents pass on a spiritual legacy to coming generations? This book deals with these issues and many

more. Also, I discuss my personal testimony and the impact of my father and mother on my upbringing that led to the ministry of Answers in Genesis, the Creation Museum, and Ark Encounter.

Answers Bible Curriculum for Sunday School and *Answers Bible Curriculum for Homeschool*

Answers in Genesis produced a unique and very powerful four-year Sunday school curriculum that teaches biblical authority and apologetics, is chronological from Genesis to Revelation, and is evangelistic. There is no other curriculum like this in the world. We have also produced a homeschool version featuring the same unique elements but designed for an at-home setting. Find out more at AnswersBibleCurriculum.com.

Answers VBS

Each year, Answers in Genesis produces a new vacation Bible school program that is evangelistic, but also teaches apologetics and biblical authority, and includes unique aspects such as science experiments and biblically based songs that teach doctrine. Find out more at AnswersVBS.com.

Answers TV

Find thousands of Answers in Genesis videos, including nature and science shows, children's programming, conferences, presentations, and so much more on the Answers in Genesis streaming platform Answers TV. Visit Answers.tv.

AnswersinGenesis.org

You can find hundreds of faith-building resources for all ages at AnswersinGenesis.org.

Answers Magazine

This award-winning quarterly publication is like two magazines in one. "Answers" features beautiful photos and illustrations that enhance amazing articles about creation, biblical authority, and how to respond to changes happening in our culture. "Kids Answers" is for the younger set, and includes awesome animal facts, games, experiments and great kid-level creation teaching! 100 pages total, delivered to your doorstep.

Visit AnswersMagazine.org/subscribe to order!